Living Passionately

Living Passionately

21 PEOPLE WHO FOUND THEIR PURPOSE— AND HOW YOU CAN TOO!

MARIA BLON, COORDINATING AUTHOR

TWO HARBORS PRESS, MINNEAPOLIS

Two Harbors Press
322 First Avenue N, 5th floor
Minneapolis, MN 55401
612.455.2293
www.TwoHarborsPress.com

This book is printed with soy-based ink.

Medical disclaimer:
The information presented in this book is offered for educational and informational purposes only, and should not be construed as personal medical advice.

ISBN-13: 978-1-63413-138-4
LCCN: 2014919275

Distributed by Itasca Books

Logo & Cover Design by Tyler DeVogel
Typeset by Mary Kristin Ross

Printed in the United States of America

I dedicate this book to people around the world who are courageously learning how to find, live and share their passions. Thank you for shining your unique light!

Maria Blon

CONTENTS

FOREWORD

Dr. Ivan Misner

I was honored when Maria Blon asked me to write the foreword for this book, not only because she is a valued, standout member of BNI® (Business Network International), the worldwide business networking organization I began back in 1985, but also because the subject matter of *Living Passionately* is particularly meaningful for me. All my life I have been a firm believer in the *Givers Gain* philosophy (put simply, it can be defined as "what goes around comes around") and I have also always adamantly believed that you may not be able to make a world of difference, but you *can* make a difference in the world. This book is solidly rooted in both of those beliefs and I feel privileged to be able to contribute to it in even a small way alongside the twenty-one coauthors who have contributed their very personal, deeply moving testaments to the resilience of the human spirit through the healing power of giving.

All of the contributing authors within these pages have found themselves at one time in a place of great challenge where most people would tend to begin thinking only of themselves and obsessing solely over how to make their own situations better. Not these people, however. Instead, they put all of their focus into finding ways to give to others what they were most desperately lacking in their own lives. As a result, they wound up receiving an amazing amount of fulfillment, purpose, and healing in return for their selflessness and generosity.

From Alison Orlando, who lost her mother at a young age and healed her grief by volunteering both locally and abroad; to Anthony Church, whose poverty-stricken childhood ignited within him a passion for entrepreneurship and a drive to find ways to help his family overcome their hardships; and on to Dr. Bradley Nelson, who learned the power of alternative healing methods as a result of his own significant health challenges and then devoted his life to teaching others around the world how to cure a wide range of illnesses through an innovative healing modality—I am endlessly inspired by the stories that fill this intriguing and empowering book.

In fact, Dr. Nelson's story and the stories of the other authors who found healing through alternative medicine are particularly resonant for me as I am now in remission from a prostate cancer diagnosis and I owe it to natural medicine and holistic healing methods. Because of that, I now run a website called MisnerPlan.com, which freely shares information about what I did to treat my cancer naturally; and I do it for the same reason these authors do what they do: to move forward with my own healing process through helping others. There really is nothing that can give you a greater sense of purpose than helping someone else in a time of serious need—especially when you can personally identify with exactly what they're going through.

I am fascinated by so many of the authors in this book who have found their sense of purpose in this way. The group of authors, for example, who went to Haiti—the poorest country in the Western Hemisphere—after a devastating earthquake had struck, and started a sustainable school (the HEART School) with the philosophy of empowering people to better their lives through education. I am also awed by the hope, courage, and depth of character displayed by authors in every stage of life such as eight-year-old Jean Widletson Gaspard and Sheila Pearl, who is in her seventies—they show us that you are never too young or too old to persevere and triumph over struggle and sorrow.

As I mentioned previously, I have always been an avid believer in the *Givers Gain* philosophy and it gives me great joy that, as the core philosophy of BNI, it is embraced by over 160,000 BNI members worldwide. Maria Blon, the editor and one of the authors of the book you're holding in your hands is one of the BNI members who truly epitomizes this philosophy. She has given the world a great gift with this book that will offer inspiration to people from all different walks of life.

Whether your life has been touched by addiction, homelessness, trauma, poverty, lack of direction, health setbacks, or other challenges, you will surely find yourself relating intimately with one story and in awe of another story. Maria's eclectic selection of authors shows her passion for inspiring many different people to follow their passions. Her reflection questions at the end of each chapter help readers to relate each story's message to their own lives and if you read the book with an open mind and heart, it will drive you to follow your own passions. Why should you put so much stock in following your passions, you ask? Well, I speak from personal experience when I say that there is no limit to the unbelievable rewards you will begin to reap when you put all your energy into doing what you are truly passionate about.

Ivan Misner, Ph.D.
New York Times bestselling author and founder of BNI

INTRODUCTION

Maria Blon

I know each story in this book will open your eyes to new possibilities for your life. I want people to live their own individual passions, not someone else's idea of how they should live. Every contributor in this book was chosen for his or her unique story and the important lessons they have to teach us all. For Jean Widletson Gaspard, Rosita Labousse and Wildo Bruny, I have added narration between passages told in their voices since they speak Haitian Creole and were interviewed for their chapters. I have also added narration between Carina Blon's blog posts.

I imagine that each person's story will touch your heart in different ways. I honor all of the contributors for their courage to be vulnerable and share their personal journeys with you. Each and every one of them has expressed a hope that their stories might help other people with their life challenges. After each story, I discuss it's lessons and then ask "reflection" questions so that you may apply what you learn to your own life.

Let us all come together in love and unity, helping ourselves and everyone around us to nurture, live and share our individual and collective passions. As you read our stories, you will relate more to some than others, and I am willing to bet that you will discover at least one remarkable kinship. While you are reading, I ask of you what I ask of all people I speak to:

- Open your mind open to possibilities.
- Keep what works and let go of the rest

A Muse for People Who Are a Work in Progress

If we consider ourselves to be "works in progress," there is never an excuse to stop working. There is never a reason to despair. We will be progressing every day toward the person we want to be. ~ Peggy Gilbart

Peggy Gilbart has a spiritual, thoughtful presence that I have long found reassuring, and so, I asked her to teach me about spirituality. She would suggest reading different books, like *Siddhartha*, and then we would discuss them, and along the way she became my first spiritual teacher. One time, while on vacation, we were walking along a path in the woods with our young children, and I was trying to get her son to move faster. Peggy asked me, "Are you in a hurry?" I thought about it and said, "No." Those few words made me realize we were on vacation, with no need to hurry. "Hurry" was simply my habit.

Peggy is also our story editor. She has not written a story in this book, but has edited and guided me and the other contributing authors through this whole process with wisdom and grace. Peggy helped me to love reading, something that I never enjoyed before. Peggy started a newsletter called "Works in Progress," which was dedicated to the improvement of self and society. She would ask for people's writing, which she gently edited, and then would start discussions amongst the readers. I thoroughly enjoyed reading—and sometimes writing for— "Works in Progress."

I feel like everyone is a work in progress, which takes the pressure off finally "getting it." Continuing to grow and learn is important to being fully engaged in life. Notice how you feel reading each of these stories. Which stories resonate the most for you? Enjoy spending time with the reflection section after each story and observe transformations as your passion is sparked and you find your purpose!

WHO AM I AND WHY DO I MATTER?

Maria Blon

I imagine this question has been asked by every person on this earth, some more often than others. I've asked myself this question many times, despite living a relatively privileged life complete with indoor plumbing, plus many recreational and educational opportunities. I write this chapter with you in mind. As you read my story, learning about my challenges and triumphs, find the threads that you connect with so that you may learn to answer these questions: *Who am I and why do I matter?* Each person in this world is here for a reason. Our individual and collective quests to be who we are and make a difference in the world *do* matter in more ways than we can even comprehend. Like most of us, my journey began when I was a small child.

Meeting and Greeting

Imagine walking up the steps to your apartment building and having two little girls, one blonde and one brunette, asking, *Where are you going? Why are you doing that?* You might also be asked the same questions by these precocious, three year old girls on the elevator or while courting your soon to be fiancée at a romantic picnic in the field near the apartments. Have you gathered that one of those chatting, curious characters was me? Yes, I was the brunette pip, with blonde sidekick, Janet. I loved spending time with my friend Janet and learning more about the people who lived in or visited our building. I am not sure that everyone was thrilled with my questions. My mother has a picture of me on her bedroom wall, taken by the young courting couple. The story goes that they photographed me, then I was encouraged to run home and tell my family that I just had my picture taken, giving the couple some peaceful time alone. I believe that I have gained a bit more awareness and tact over the years, yet I continue to meet new people wherever I travel, asking, *Where are you going? Why are you doing that?* Some of these stories are on my blog PeopleLivingPassionately.com, where you can read about the many interesting friends I have made on my travels. When my youngest daughter Anna was 4 years old, she asked me wide eyed, "Mommy, do you know *everyone* in the whole world?" Oh the joy of children's innocent questions! In Anna's world, I did know everyone since I say hello to each person that I pass when walking and enjoy chatting with people who cross my path.

Who am I and why do I matter?

I am a People Greeter. I matter by showing people they are important because I am interested in them, often bringing smiles to their faces.

Who are you and why do you matter?

I know that you are a person I would love to meet and get to know. You have come to this earth to help in an important way. If you are not yet certain of what your passion or purpose is, clues are often found in your childhood. Remember what you really loved and didn't like as a child, back before people and other influences guided you away from your true self. What did you dream of as a child? Are you living some of your dreams? Each day is a new beginning and an opportunity to live passionately, one step at a time. Begin by remembering your passions as a child today.

Volunteering

Since I started Kindergarten at only four years old, I was younger than my classmates and felt a little out of it socially throughout school. I didn't feel comfortable at parties, especially if there was drinking or drugs. Being physically active, singing and playing outside with friends was where I felt most at home. Luckily, my parents loved being outside in the woods and especially near water so that we could swim and my dad could fish. I thrived on being involved with groups where I could be a part of something bigger than myself, because this made me feel important. I was an active Girl Scout until I was a teenager. With my troop, I not only went on grand outdoor adventures like caving, white water rafting and rock climbing, but also volunteered in a variety of places. I especially enjoyed assisting with the recycling program, where we sorted glass bottles by colors and metals by their type. I felt great when I helped make the earth just a little bit cleaner and more sustainable.

When I was thirteen, our family went on vacation to the island of Newfoundland so that my father could go salmon fishing. Even though I loved being in nature, camping in the middle of an island with no hot water or social life was not my idea of a fun vacation. I met an important person on that trip, a mysterious bearded man who arrived on bicycle at dusk. My brother Paul and I were eager to meet our camping neighbor when we saw his fire blazing on this dark and lonely night. Just like when I was 3 years old, we ventured over to greet this person. He was a school teacher, married to a woman he adored and shared fascinating stories of his summer bicycle adventures. I felt very strongly, with great certainty: *This is the kind of man I want to marry because he loves his wife, job and adventures!* I thoroughly enjoyed this evening, then the man took off on his bike the next morning and I didn't think about him until years later.

After our trip to Newfoundland, Girl Scouts was over and I floundered to figure out where I fit in, which was such a scary and lonely time for me. My strongest longing, which I didn't share with anyone, not even my best girl friend at the time, was to find a soul mate, a man to share my life with. I wasn't willing to date anyone that didn't feel like the right match. While I waited for this perfect person to come into my life, I was lucky enough to be welcomed with open arms to join an active church youth group. I can't imagine what would have happened if I didn't find this group. We had thought provoking discussions, during which our leader, Renny Domske encouraged us to speak our mind and ask probing questions. He empowered us to figure out what made sense to each of us as individuals, which was and still is, so very important to me. We were an active group, playing line volleyball (no net, just a line, which meant some wicked spikes) and went on mission trips. We performed for the churches we visited on our journey from Pittsburgh, through Canada, all the way to the Maine coast I remember our performances vividly to this day: jumping off the stage, turning around, then leaping up while we sang a praise song together. When we were renovating a retreat center, Renny knew that I liked to be physical and do exciting things, so he placed me with the boys to shingle a roof. How empowering this was for fiercely independent me, to be given a job in a typically male role. I felt like I was on top of the world, and in that little community, I literally was. I didn't find my soul mate in this group, but felt embraced by these people, which was an incredible blessing to me.

In the often confusing teen years, these opportunities to feel part of a group and volunteer were invaluable for me and helped shape who I am today. Thank you to everyone empowering teens, as they are finding their unique path in life.

Who am I and why do I matter?

I am an Eager Volunteer, helping myself, people and the earth when I offer service in our local and global community. I matter because I care and am doing my best to make a difference, one project at a time.

Who are you and why do you matter?

You have something important to offer, which is uniquely yours. What are you here to give or receive? What kinds of volunteer work have you enjoyed? Are there youth in your life who could benefit from your encouragement to be of service in their community?

Are you struggling in some area of your life? There are individuals and groups who are eager to assist you. By allowing yourself to receive help, you are empowering people to feel good about themselves.

Choosing a Career

I felt so much pressure in my teen years to decide on what I wanted to do for the rest of my life. Honestly, why is so much pressure put on teens to make these big decisions instead of giving them time to explore life and their passions? I took career interest tests, thinking maybe they could give me the magical answer I was looking for, so when yet another person asked the dreaded question, *What will you be studying in college?* I was able to give some kind of answer at least close to what I might enjoy and be good at. I was not a confident writer when I was young, which was frustrating because I always wanted to do my best. In fact, I used to be so afraid of writing in high school that I would put off my papers to the very last minute and then, due to the time crunch, I had no choice but to write the paper or fail the class. I remember setting my alarm for 4 am to begin a paper due on the same day. I put myself through undue stress because I allowed my writing anxiety to paralyze me, instead of considering other options like writing an outline or setting a small goal for each day leading up to the deadline. Needless to say, I didn't choose journalism as my major in college. Fortunately, I worked through my writing anxiety in college by simply getting out what I wanted to say, knowing I could edit later. Now, with computers, I can pour my soul onto the page and even my spelling is corrected. How miraculous is that?

I did well in mathematics throughout school because I worked hard and studied every day, a key to success in mathematics. In my freshman year of college, I discovered that I enjoyed tutoring fellow students in math because I found I was able to ease their anxiety, encouraging them to believe in their ability to succeed by teaching them what I had learned over the years. I then decided to try teaching math as a career, so began my education at Penn State University where I earned my bachelor's degree in mathematics with a minor in computer science. This was a huge confidence boost for me career wise, but more importantly I met my soul mate, Tom Blon when I was traveling on the bus for a home visit. We chatted a little bit on the ride home, then he sat next to me when we headed back to college and we talked the whole trip, my heart so full of a new amazing feeling of giddy excitement and yes, passion. I knew this was the man for me and we spent time with each other every day since that bus ride. Tom did eventually become a teacher and loves to bike just like the man I met in Newfoundland on that dark and lonely night four years earlier. I was truly a lucky, lucky person of just seventeen because I had found my soul mate who I loved and still love so completely. I know many people struggle to find loving relationships and for this blessing in my life, I am very grateful. Tom and I were married on July 25, 1987, one year after we graduated from Penn State.

I was still baffled by the next step on my career quest. I wanted to start teaching right away, but felt pressured into earning my master's degree in pure mathematics, which I tried twice but failed miserably both times. I did not feel passionate about that level of math and had no motivation whatsoever. I made a choice to follow my passion for teaching. I quickly and seemingly effortlessly earned my master's degree from George Washington University in math education, graduating with a perfect 4.0. I learned during those years how important it was for me to do what I am passionate about. When I do, I am much happier and more successful. Thankfully, I stopped listening to other people and followed my intuition. I began my professional career teaching mathematics at community colleges in my own unique way.

I loved teaching in hands-on, interactive ways. I learned to coach my students to reach the goals they set for themselves, and to evaluate their own progress. I required my math students to do a lot of writing, along with mathematics in my classes. Students who thought they would never be successful in math (maybe you can relate) overcame their anxiety, building confidence and new life skills. I firmly believed anyone could learn mathematics if they were willing to practice daily and were taught in creative ways. I expanded from teaching arithmetic through calculus classes, to instructing future elementary students how to teach using hands-on, interactive methods. I became a mentor for future teachers. With the help of my fellow teachers and interested students, we started the Future Teacher's Association (FTA), a club whose members volunteered to support a variety of educational causes, organized lectures for the campus, went on trips to learn about education, and much more. Each semester, the FTA was guided by the student leadership. We led faculty and students campus wide to create an interactive hands-on learning display. Each visitor was welcomed by beautiful posters with inspirational quotes on stunning nature scenes, suspended from the vaulted ceiling. How lucky I was to be teaching in a place where I could bring a community together to create, encourage and share innovative teaching.

Despite all of these wonderful accomplishments, there was a part of me that didn't feel like I fit in, which was rather lonely. This may be surprising to people who knew me then. I wasn't sure how to talk about that empty feeling inside, so continued to smile and greet people as I walked on campus. Every now and then, I am reminded that I did make an impact during these years. I was getting on a plane the other day and heard a voice calling, *Mrs. Blon, Mrs. Blon.* I saw a student that I had about 15 years ago, a tall strapping man who had squeezed into the desk/chair in the front row of my basic math class. He had been there every day, looking eager, scared and hopeful that this time maybe he could get it right and succeed in math. I don't know what circumstances in life had scared him so around math, but this look was very familiar to me. Succeed he did and when I spoke with him on the plane he kept repeating what a wonderful teacher I was and how I helped him to succeed in math. I may not have felt like I completely fit in teaching math, but at that moment on the plane, I knew that my life had meaning because I was able to help this amazing man to believe in himself and his ability to succeed. This was an important stepping stone in his life and I am proud to have played a part.

Who am I and why do I matter?

I am an Interactive Teacher, encouraging individuals to find the best way to learn and encouraging teachers to share their innovative teaching strategies. I matter because every student deserves to learn in a way that empowers him or her to reach their full potential.

Who are you and why do you matter?

How did you decide on your present career? Do you feel passionate and inspired by your job? If yes, wonderful. If no, it is never too late to make a change. You will be reading about how I made career changes as my passions shifted and expanded.

I Want to Do More

After my daughter Carina was born, I started to wonder: *Am I doing enough? Shouldn't I be doing more to help people—something bigger than just teaching mathematics?*

When heated discussions arose at the college about the large number of underprepared students, I jumped at the chance to help solve this multifaceted problem. I had no experience with the politics of making positive changes at an institution. Little did I know what I was getting myself into . . . . I naively interpreted venting and complaining to be a call for action and wrongly assumed we would have a lot of supporters. We had a small, dedicated group of hard working people who were counselors, faculty and administrators. We proposed incorporating college success courses to help incoming students, by teaching study skills, time management, money management, and values clarification, plus how to set and achieve goals.

The best part of the whole experience was being trained as a college success teacher because I learned so much about myself in the process. I went to Washington, DC, to attend David Ellis's training, centered on his book *The Master Student*. I discovered the power of music to travel deep into our souls, leading us to life transformation. My passion for motivating people through music has become such a joy. I can clearly feel myself in that large training room filled with people, the lights down low and listening to Garth Brooks' song *The River*. These lines especially stood out to me:

> *So don't you sit upon the shoreline*
> *And say you're satisfied*
> *Choose to chance the rapids*
> *And dare to dance the tide . . . yes*
> *I will sail my vessel*
> *Til the river runs dry. . .*

I would sing this and other inspiring songs in my car as I drove, envisioning the day when students would have a course to help them find what they were meant to study, learning to be successful college students, while they transformed into happy, passionate people. I will forever be grateful to Dr. Preston Pulliams, the president of the college at the time, who took me under his wing to teach me about politics and leadership. He showed me how to create a vision, mission and values statement, and invited me to meet other college presidents and coordinators of college success programs. He introduced me to Stephen Covey's book, *The 7*

Habits of Highly Successful People.

Despite the wonderful support I received, we ran into a lot of resistance when attempting to get the college success program started. After a tremendous amount of dedication and hard work, my vision did not become reality. I was crushed. I took all the blame for the failure. I tried to shrug it off, to continue teaching and caring for my family, but there were days when I could barely get up in the morning. I would call in sick to work and take Carina to the babysitter, thinking I had a serious physical illness. I realize, now, that I was deeply depressed, which I was able to work through over time and with the help of family, friends and my counselor Bill Harker. I realized by putting so much importance on this program succeeding, I forgot the really important parts of life like appreciating my family and taking time to enjoy life.

Despite all the struggles, I never gave up. Years later, a college success course was accepted into the curriculum, and I was able to teach a few classes. With the help of many people, including the wise leadership of our new Vice President Catherine Chew, I also helped start a learning community program, which included a college success class. The river never went completely dry. I learned a tremendous amount through this whole process.

When my youngest daughter Anna was born, I was searching for a way to feel more peaceful and confident. I was once again ready to learn something new and began studying yoga. I gained strength, flexibility, balance, confidence and focus. Since yoga gave me so many wonderful benefits, I wanted to share this newfound passion and deepen my practice, so I trained to be a yoga teacher. I traveled around the country to earn my YogaFit teacher training certificate and had a fantastic time. I was lucky that Tom encouraged me to branch out and continue learning while he took care of our young girls during my travels. Now, the question was, where would I teach? With the help once again of Catherine Chew, I was able to teach yoga as a physical education class at the community college. I felt blessed that Catherine believed in helping students learn holistically and was able to help me through the entrenched academic political maze that resists innovation and change. Students loved de-stressing in my yoga classes and I was happy to teach them tools to bring more balance in their lives.

Who am I and why do I matter?

I am a Change Agent, encouraging people to look beyond the way that life is now and consider new possibilities. I matter because with support, I have the optimism and courage to lead people and institutions to try something new, expanding their horizons. Even if I don't achieve my full vision, I am planting seeds that may grow when the time is right.

Who are you and why do you matter?

You know that life could be better than it is now. What is most important to you? Where would you like to have an impact? Start by making changes to your life first. When you are ready to branch out to help people in your community, begin with small steps, connecting in a way that excites you, creating a better life for yourself and everyone around you.

Career jump

My father's death in November 2010 was a turning point for me. He had a longtime habit of questioning me and I think I allowed his critical voice to impede my decision-making at times. When he passed away, I felt the freedom to take a leap of faith and leave my twenty-year career of community college teaching to study Phoenix Rising Yoga Therapy and start my business, "Create Your Wellness".

Phoenix Rising Yoga Therapy is a combination of assisted yoga postures paired with reflecting the client's experiences through Rogerian dialogue. This type of dialogue is based on the philosophy that individuals have the ability to solve their own problems if they can hear what they are saying repeated back to them in a safe environment. Using this technique with clients, I learned a great deal about working intimately with people, creating a healing environment, assessing needs, sensing therapeutic moments, all while communicating verbally and non-verbally. This was also a time of deep emotional, physical and spiritual healing for me. I looked at habits that were not serving me, like keeping my feelings locked inside rather than listening to the wisdom they had to offer me. Taking time to be quiet and reflective, while scary initially, helped me to understand myself better. I learned to accept myself for who I was. I spent a lot of time meditating, doing yoga, writing and being in nature. This introspective learning allowed me to teach people to understand themselves. During this transformational time, I met my healing friend, Melanie, who you will read about in her chapter.

I sought and received a lot of support during this time, ranging from regular massages to energy healing and coaching. Meeting Rev. Dechen Rheault and receiving healing from her has given me the confidence to understand more deeply who I am and why I am here.

I met Dechen in Bristol, Vermont when I was taking Phoenix Rising Yoga Therapy training. Dechen is a petite woman who humbly scuttled in and out at lunch breaks to give us chair massages. She gave anyone interested an introductory five minute session. I so enjoyed receiving massages from Dechen during breaks. I also noticed Dechen's business card on the bulletin board and her titles: CMT (Certified Massage Therapist), Reiki Teacher, Seer. I didn't know what a seer was. I was intrigued and quite frankly a bit scared. I saw other people getting a Life Reading from Dechen after our class that day. I decided to take a leap of faith and schedule a reading as well. I still have the little piece of paper that I took notes on dated August 2010. Here is what I wrote down:

There is violet light, angelic spiritual energy around you. We need more people like you on this earth. You will use the tools of Circle, Giving and Receiving to set the stage for people to transform. Your medicine is deep and big. You will do energy work integrating Father Sky and Mother Earth and the five elements. You also have a higher medicine and power. It is important that you not feel responsible if people "get it" or not. You can observe but not feel responsible. You can accomplish anything. You question yourself, "Who do I think I am?" because you came into this life not believing in yourself. You can step into knowing your role when you set fear aside. You will do a lot of travel and will learn to balance your family with travel. Test the waters so that you will see you can be attentive to family and also travel. Know that you can say whatever you need to say with great compassion. You are on your path. Spirit is working with you. You are a divine and humble being. There is nowhere to go, your path will unfold. You have nothing to prove. You will know your place in the circle of life. When sitting with people, bow to the person's love and power. Remember to return to your breathing. You will become an apprentice and learn through a teacher, around a year from now.

As I continued to connect with and receive healing from Dechen, I admired her humility, honesty and spiritual mastery. I remember wondering how I was going to find a teacher, thinking that I would have to travel to meet them. As it turns out, Dechen is my Spiritual teacher. I learn from each reading and healing that she gives me either in person or over the phone. She has taught me meditation and healing techniques, plus Reiki levels one and two. I learn at my own pace, in my own time, which is so important to me. I feel like Dechen guides me to become my best self, not her idea of who I should be. I feel so blessed. I think Dechen should be much more famous than she is with over 40 years of healing experience and mastery. I feel honored that Dechen is my patient, humble, masterful teacher, guiding me peacefully to follow my passions.

During this time of healing, I began teaching my own yoga classes, renting a beautiful circular room at a church, as well as teaching once a week at a medical facility to their staff. I was lucky to meet Sheila Pearl, an experienced entrepreneur, who taught me about networking and courageously re-creating myself. I learned about marketing and healing, which has been both terrifying and exciting. Can you relate to feeling excited and terrified when learning and expanding your horizons?

Who am I and why do I matter?

I am a Brave Explorer, traveling deep inside my soul to discover why I am here and how I can be of service. I matter because I am a model for reflection, self-exploration and sharing my learning so that people may find themselves.

Who are you and why do you matter?

Have you taken time to do some soul searching, to ask yourself, why am I here? What is my role? Identify supportive people in your life and lean on them as you discover yourself. You are here for a reason and do matter. Carve out some time every day to be quiet, to pray, meditate, be in nature, write, whatever is calling you the most. Schedule time to simply be, not to produce but to enjoy relaxing and getting away from your everyday routines. You will open your mind to new possibilities.

Time to Travel

Leaving my full-time position at the college also gave me the freedom to travel. I never would have predicted I would go to Haiti, a country I knew very little about. Why Haiti? My daughter Carina had wanted to volunteer her service in a third world country for some time. When Carina was on a tour of colleges with her friends, Guidance Counselor Shad St Louis showed video footage of his trip to Haiti right after the devastating earthquake of January 2010. Carina asked Shad if she could go on his next trip. He said that, since she was not yet eighteen, one of her parents would have to go with her. Carina gave a big sigh, her shoulders and head drooped down low for a few seconds, then she perked up and said, "Mommy, will you go with me?" I said yes, and our adventure began in July 2010.

I had never been to a third world country, much less soon after a natural disaster. Flying into Haiti and viewing the shocking contrast of Haiti's brown barren mountains, stripped of trees due to desperation of the people needing wood for cooking, compared with the lush green mountains of the Dominican Republic was—and continues to be—a deep source of sadness for me, since I love being in green, lush nature. The cheerful attitudes of the survivors I met were amazing to me. They were grateful and welcoming, taking time to ask me how I was doing. I asked myself, if people can be upbeat right after a devastating disaster, why did I complain about my challenges that were relatively small in comparison? I learned to be grateful and appreciate all that I have at my home in New York. The drive from the airport in Port au Prince was overwhelming when I saw people living in tents at the side of a busy highway, where they bathed in public because they had no choice. My heart sank at the sight of garbage clogging the rivers. Toxic smoke from burning garbage stung my eyes. Since there were no garbage or recycling trucks to collect their waste, everything was put in a big pile: plastic, batteries and diapers. You name it, they burned it. Besides the garbage and the medical care issues, transportation was an ordeal and sanitation was primitive. In the United States, we have electricity, which is on all the time. In Haiti, electricity was off more than it was on. With unemployment in Haiti at over 70%, too many people do not have the ability to find meaningful work. So many problems. *Where do we begin solving these problems?* Sorting through all of my feelings was challenging. During our week-long visit, I was tough on the outside, but, inside, I was all torn up. When I am confused, one strategy I use to feel better is to make my environment more orderly. This was a big challenge in Haiti.

I wanted so much to do something to help. Inside, I was screaming, *can't we fix this awful mess right now?* I quietly went to the garbage pile at the back of the home where we were camping and starting sorting the organic materials out to create a compost pile. Nobody would help or go near me. They were wise. I got bitten by ants, and the bites turned into terrible infections. I didn't go to the doctor for several days after returning home until it got really bad. I reasoned, the people in Haiti don't have medical care, so why did I deserve to see the doctor? What I didn't consider is they probably had immunities to some infections that I did not. It took me a while to recover from that trip to Haiti. I learned that there were some problems too big for me to even begin finding a solution. How silly of me to think that I could solve the garbage problem in Haiti. Did I have any training or experience whatsoever in waste management, other than maintaining our little compost pile at home or volunteering to sort bottles for recycling? No. I am living and learning with each new experience.

Again, I asked, a little more experienced this time, *Where do we begin solving these problems?* Guided by Shad and Carina's leadership, we began with the children through education. Since teaching is my area of expertise, this made a lot of sense, to focus in on what I know, in order to have the biggest impact, one step at a time. You will read about building the HEART School in Haiti in Carina and Shad's chapters.

When we volunteered in Haiti, we lived among the Haitian people, near to, on top of or in Shad's family's house. On our first trip, we camped on the ground, the next trip, we climbed a rickety ladder to a roof, where we slept in tents. We took bucket showers with cold water hand pumped from a well, which was a 60 foot walk from the shower on a muddy path in a sugar cane field. The bathroom was outside, so anyone needing to go there in the middle of the night went down the rickety ladder in the dark, sometimes encountering a tarantula on the way. With each visit, there was more room, order and conveniences. There is now a well with a pump that works when the electricity is on. There are concrete stairs going up to the roof, which now has a beautiful palm house, complete with running water (albeit cold), a tile floor, bunk beds, and even furniture. Mimi the kitten patrols Shad's property for mice, rats, and rogue moths that dare enter her domain. The fridge works when the electricity is on. Cooking is done on charcoal—which is a whole other discussion because of the effects cooking with charcoal has on the land and people's health. I continue to be intrigued by the way that people live in Haiti, sometimes feeling like I am in a time warp, having traveled back to colonial days, when people pressed clothes using an iron filled with charcoal for heat.

To date, I have been to Haiti a total of eight times, where I have helped in a number of different ways. My favorite trip was in January 2014, because I interviewed Rosita, Gaspard and Wildo for this book and trained the teachers at the HEART elementary school. I was giving within my areas of expertise and passion, which felt fantastic because I knew that I was doing my very best I am so excited for you to have the opportunity to read and be inspired by our Haitian authors' stories.

Our trips have not only been about helping but also exploring the lush, green, resorts on this island country, where flowers bloom, palm trees sway in the ocean breeze and mouthwatering food is abundant. Escaping for a day to swim, relax and enjoy delicious food at Kaliko Beach with the guys that provided security and so much help to us was a wonderful treat. On one trip, we splurged and treated Carina, Shad, Anna and myself to three days at the beautiful tropical resort: Moulin Sur Mer. Shad and Carina received a well-deserved break from all of their hard work. Anna and I enjoyed living in luxury that we had never experienced before: a tropical beach with water trampoline, monkeys that we chatted with every day, beautiful gardens, delicious Haitian food and a traditional Carnaval celebration. This vacation not only renewed our spirits but also gave us hope for Haiti transforming into a tropical paradise, which is welcoming and nourishing to both tourists and its beautiful native people.

Who am I and why do I matter?

I am a Humanitarian, who has reached beyond my immediate community to help our poorest third world neighbors in Haiti. Simply by visiting and speaking with the people, showing them that I care and their lives are important, I am making a difference. Offering my expertise in education and sharing Haitian people's stories through this book are added bonuses. I know how vitally important it is for me to take care of myself, while reaching out to help.

Who are you and why do you matter?

Simply being yourself and living passionately brings positive energy to everyone around you. There are so many worthy causes in the world. Which cause do you feel most drawn to help? Maybe you will be guided to lend support in a place that you might never expect. Take some time to notice what pulls at your heartstrings, exploring options of helping in your community and beyond. Focusing on what you feel most called to is important, because you will be able to give the best of yourself while staying healthy.

Back to Business

Still, I felt there was more for me to explore—I decided to learn about energy healing, beginning with Reiki, then Integrated Energy Therapy (IET), followed by The Emotion Code. As you have probably gathered, I love to keep learning, yet struggle with how to incorporate everything I enjoy into my career. I went through a confusing time, two years after leaving the college, when I decided to switch from my original business "Create Your Wellness" and opened my new company, "SPARKS!" I loved my yoga students, and saying goodbye to them was very hard. I helped yoga teachers in my area by referring students to them, which felt great. While those days of uncertainty were horribly uncomfortable and scary, they were essential for me to expand and grow. Native American cultures refer to these times as "the dark night of the soul". I am grateful for my husband Tom's support and stability during those challenging days. My brother, Paul, and his wife Rae have been wonderful role models of following an entrepreneurial dream and succeeding. What I wanted most of all was for people, including myself, to shed thoughts and feelings that they didn't believe, to figure out who they really were, in order to live passionate and fulfilling lives. I was learning as I was building my new business. With SPARKS, I began creating interactive classes, incorporating a variety of different modalities.

I had only two years business experience, felt very scared about this new venture and wanted to connect with entrepreneurs for support and encouragement. I wanted two women and two men in what we called the Business Inspiration Group (BIG). I invited my friend Ann Bell, Anthony Church and Brian Baird to meet at least once a month for more than a year. You will learn a bit more about each of these people in this book. Our group was a place where we all felt safe to say, "I don't know what the heck I am doing and I am open to ideas." Once the issues were on the table, we helped each other to see our strengths and find solutions. Each meeting had an agenda with time boundaries. We began by each person taking a full meeting to:

- Introduce their business while everyone listened,
- Answer questions from the group, and
- Listen while each group member gave us suggestions. During this time, we were not allowed to say, "I tried that and it failed." Or "I can't do that." We simply listened, as challenging as that could be.

The following meeting, the person who presented the last time would share what he or she had learned and implemented from the previous meeting and a new person would present his or her business. After everyone presented, we created themes for discussion, even helping each other build a Vision, Mission, and Values statement. These meetings were rich with honesty, depth, and a sincere desire to help each other succeed in "life first, business also."

With Ann Bell, I co-created classes and inspiration cards to help people discover themselves through meditation, movement, and motivation. I love being inspired through my work, while meeting new and interesting people. As a result of my studies and creations, I find myself able to offer people a great deal more than before. The more I do what I am passionate about, the better I am at it.

Now a whole line of SPARKS products have been created with the eight themes of Perspective, Joy, Gratitude, Courage, Hope, Vision, Perseverance, and Presence:

- Eight-week Online and In-person Inspiration Class.
- Inspiration Card Deck with thirty-two different cards, plus journal.
- Aromatherapy and Crystal Sets.
- Kindle books: *Live an Inspired Live* and *Inspiration Stories*

What wonderful accomplishments! But, these products do not sell themselves, and marketing was a great challenge for me. I remember going to my first big outdoor fair after having a banner and fliers created, and spending lots of time making and creating the aromatherapy and crystal sets. I was so excited to share these beautiful healing products. Tom joined me on the first day of the fair, which was so hot and humid, sweat dripped down our faces while we simply stood still. I sold some artwork to raise money for the HEART School in Haiti and made a connection for my friend Alison Orlando, but I did not sell one SPARKS product the entire day. I was devastated and cried the whole next morning before heading back to the fair. I shed my last few tears in the car, thinking about my counselor, Bill Harker, from years earlier, who said I put so much of my heart into creating for people, he worried I would not be appreciated and my feelings would be hurt. Interestingly enough, I ran into Bill and his wife that morning. I didn't share my struggles, but instead talked about what Carina was up to in Haiti. I wanted to be mature and handle this challenge with courage, while allowing Bill and his wife to enjoy the day. That second day went pretty well. I sold one set of SPARKS Inspiration cards, more Haitian artwork, and made some lovely connections.

I continued to persevere, attending wellness fairs and vendor expos over the summer, having more luck each time. I learned to engage customers with raffles, singing monkeys and creating a display from which people could sample the aromatherapy oils. How humbling it was to put myself out there time after time, without receiving much profit. I imagine many new entrepreneurs can relate to how I was feeling.

I still had much to learn about leading a successful business, so was very lucky to discover BNI (Business Network International), which has taught me entrepreneurial skills through my local BNI Profit Makers weekly group, and the extended local and global network. I have learned to grow my business and help my group members grow their businesses through referrals. The BNI *Givers Gain* philosophy matches my values perfectly. Basically, when we are generous by helping people, that goodwill returns to us. In other words, we reap what we sow. My lively personality and quirky presentations brought life to our weekly meetings. I have felt so loved, accepted, and appreciated by this group, plus their businesses have helped my business to grow. Here are some examples of how BNI members have helped SPARKS grow:

- Anthony Church of Blue Buckle Marketing is the reason you are reading this book today, due to his extensive marketing expertise and encouragement. He also took my SPARKS Inspiration Class to learn more about my business. Anthony's friendship and humanitarianism are great sources of inspiration for me.
- Frank DeRaffle, our BNI regional leader and a contributing author of the *New York Times* bestseller *Business Networking and Sex*, has guided me in the publishing and speaking world through his Entrepreneurial Excellence Program. Also, he connected me with Dr. Ivan Misner who wrote our beautiful foreword.
- Greg Miller of CMIT Solutions keeps my computer running and my files backed up. When my computer crashed a year ago, he was able to retrieve all of my files, saving many SPARKS creations.
- Erni Hewett of Erni Girl Designs designed the SPARKS Inspi-

ration cards, which are now flying off the shelves of many stores, plus she organized her book group to write reviews for this book.

- Connie Wehmeyer of Subtle Energies created the formulas for the SPARKS aromatherapy oils.
- Alison Orlando, a certified health coach with Take Shape For Life has helped me find places to teach and promote my business countless times, encouraged me to keep going, plus she has taken my classes.
- Charles Yarnold of Focused Wealth Management has earned more money for my retirement than I have with SPARKS so far. Charles also took my SPARKS Inspiration Class and helped me to be a keynote speaker at a Caregiver's Conference.
- A visitor to our BNI group referred Wendy Blanchard to me. I feel so lucky to have helped Wendy with her recovery and to be a part of her mission to educate people about—and to overcome—mental illness and addiction through her business, The Rx Diaries.
- Deborah Cohen, life coach with Peaceful Thunder Coaching from the New Paltz BNI group, has helped me tremendously with her creative coaching and encouragement.

Many more people have helped me through BNI and I am eternally grateful for their encouragement and support. For a long time, I have felt this way about my husband Tom and his unconditional love, but never before have I felt this way toward a group of people. Being part of a community of entrepreneurs has been essential to maintain hope during the lows and highs on my entrepreneurial adventures.

Each member of a BNI group has the opportunity to hold a position. I thoroughly enjoyed being the Education Coordinator. Each week, I shared tips for members to grow their business. I was learning myself as I was teaching. During the creation stage of SPARKS, I did not have many clients, and having to find something positive to say when I was terrified and uncertain whether my new business would succeed was excellent therapy. I learned that addressing challenges while staying positive is vital to maintaining motivation.

Who am I and why do I matter?

I am an Adventurous Entrepreneur who helps people, through many different methods, to discover their passions so that they can live an inspired life. I know that I need support when learning new skills, so I gather people together or join experienced groups that teach me what I need to learn. I matter because I care about people and am willing to take risks.

Who are you and why do you matter?

Is there a business that you would like to start? What problem will you be helping people solve? What information and skills will you need to learn in order to be successful? I am asking many questions here because it makes a huge difference when you answer these questions, then look for support to make your business dreams come true. Maybe you are not interested in becoming an entrepreneur and that is completely okay. As always, keep what works for you and let go of the rest. You make a difference by being your authentic self in every area of your life.

Inspiring People

I enjoy teaching a small group of people in an intimate setting and getting to know them well, but I really love inspiring large groups of people as a keynote presenter because this gives me the opportunity to help as many more people. I had a wonderful time being the keynote speaker at a Caregiver's Conference in Kingston, New York. I created an interactive presentation, during which audience members learned the three M's in a way that related to their caregiving challenges:

✓ Motivation: I shared quick stories of my experiences and learning as a caregiver for my youngest brother, Evan, and how I learned at a young age how important it was for me to take care of myself and continue enjoying life while caregiving. Participants were guided to compare and contrast their personality with the person they were caring for. Pockets of laughter burst out around the room.

✓ Movement: Using an entertaining scene from the movie, *The*

Intouchables, everyone in the room got up to move their bodies to the music and enjoy some fun. Some people are afraid to dance in public, but I create a safe atmosphere by dancing in goofy ways that make people laugh and want to join in.

✓ Meditation: I called this the mystery M at first and had slips of paper around the room which people volunteered to read about the benefits of, they guessed it, meditation. We turned the lights down low and I led the group in a short meditation, which was many people's favorite part of the presentation.

The person who presented after me mumbled that I was a tough act to follow. Organizers of this conference were thrilled that I inspired participants to let go and enjoy themselves while learning valuable tools to help them live a more balanced life. Everyone who attends one of my talks leaves with a smile on their face and a new perspective for their life. I share what has worked for me and what has been a big flop. We laugh a lot, but most important, I give participants a chance to experience themselves in a new way through short meditations or breathing exercises, moving to a fun song and sharing their ideas with a neighbor. Each presentation is unique and tailored to the needs and interests audience. I enjoy encouraging participants to use the LOVE formula, which has helped me transform over the years:

> **Let go…**
> **Open your mind**
> **Vision**
> **Experience Everything**

This cycle may be started at any place, depending on where you are on your journey.

❖ *Let Go...*

Is there something in your life that is not serving you, yet you are holding on because it feels comfortable and familiar? Keeping what is not working may feel easier in the short run, but can create so much heart-ache in the long run. Have you ever missed the day when trash pick-up in the summer and garbage sits in the hot can for two weeks? We did and oh, the smell, the flies, how disgusting. When I keep garbage in my life, it stinks and infects every aspect of my being. Taking time to clarify what I really want to keep and let go of what isn't serving me, I feel relieved and make space for something new and better. This process of letting go can be emotional, first with uncertainty and then with relief. Whew! Life is always changing and I am learning to embrace these changes with less drama. A great way to physically let go is to dance. Put on fun music, move and enjoy!

❖ *Open your mind*

This is a place to not have expectations and say: "I am ready, bring on the ideas." Try this simple exercise:

- Breathe in through your nose and tense the muscles in your face, then
- Breathe out through your mouth and release the tension.

How does your face feel? Continue to tense and release while breathing, working all the way down your body in this way. Spend a few minutes sitting and notice your breathing. When your mind wanders (like mine often does), bring your attention gently back to your breath. Taking time for this simple practice is a great way to start your day with clarity and peace. From this place of receptivity, you are setting the stage for

❖ *Vision*

Create a vison for your life that lifts your spirits, making your heart sing with joy! How, you ask? One way is to create a vision board, which is a collage of your life's passions and dreams. This is a wonderful activity because it encourages you to be creative and clarify what you really want in life. I enjoy guiding people to create vision boards in my classes. Here is a SPARKS Inspiration Card to get you started in a small way:

Vision!

I am lacking direction and purpose in my life. I feel stuck and don't know how to move forward.

Healing:

Look through magazines that I have. When I see a picture that inspires me, cut it out and put it in a place where I will see it often today. Let this picture inspire my day!

Affirmation:

I expand my horizons, creating a new vision for my life!

~ Maria Blon & Ann Bell

❖ *Experience Everything*

Both the high and low points on your journey arrive to teach you lessons. Pay attention during challenges, feeling and learning from everything. Notice when you are afraid to move forward. Take time to discern, is this a rational fear which should be paid attention to, or is this an irrational fear which should be ignored in order to press on courageously? Celebrate each little and big success, feeling the exhilaration of victory.

I have used this formula to transform my life and I hope that you will achieve great success using the LOVE formula. During times of transition, I sometimes worry too much about succeeding and judge some projects as failures because I didn't reach my initial goals. Dechen assures me that I am learning through each project, and when I am not interested in something anymore, it is time to move on, because the lesson is done and will help me in my next creation. Most of all, scheduling time for fun is so important. Luckily, my parents took us on many outdoor adventures. Whether sledding, swimming, parasailing, skiing, jumping in puddles, laughing, dancing or creating, I like the feeling of freedom and flow, which comes through play.

Even the prayer I say each morning before meditating is playful:

I am grateful for this time to release and embrace all that encourages me to dance through life with wisdom and passion, helping people all along the way. This is good, we are grateful.

Who am I and why do I matter?

I am an Inspirational Speaker who revels in opening people's minds to new possibilities and potentials. I love transforming a room of people into a space where individuals feel safe to share their stories, dance, meditate and view their life from a new and enlightening perspective. I matter because too many people feel unfulfilled and unhappy. I have the tools to help people love themselves, shine brighter and light up the whole world with their passions!

Who are you and why do you matter?

You matter because you are you, a unique person with something beautiful to offer us all and I hope to meet you someday soon.

Writing

I started writing my story 4 years ago, when leaving my long time career of teaching at the community college and going through a lot of healing. Getting my thoughts and feelings onto paper or the computer screen helped me make sense of what was happening and served as a release. I intended to publish my story at that time, but something didn't feel right. In the fall of 2013, the idea of asking people to write their stories as part of this book emerged and my excitement increased with each person's story. My chapter was the first one started, but was also the last one to be finished. I struggled with telling a story that would be interesting for people to read, which was embarrassing to me as the coordinating author. Thanks to guidance from Peggy, Tom, the editors at Mill City Press and reading my coauthor's stories, I learned that great writers bring readers into their world by describing what they are feeling and thinking. I was extremely relieved and highly motivated when at the last minute this theme emerged: *Who am I and why do I matter?* Since I am helping you while sharing my story, writing has much greater meaning for me. Every person matters and has something amazing to offer!

I feel so alive when discussing people's stories and learning about their lives. I have an extra sparkle in my eye and a bounce in my step that wasn't there before. I know this is what I am meant to be doing in my life: encouraging people to find, live, and share their passions. I've been using writing as a tool to help people throughout my life, first as a math, college success, and yoga teacher, an energy healer, then as a life coach, inspirational speaker and now as a coordinating author.

Many thanks to every single person who has cheered me on and contributed to this book. I truly hope these stories will be read by millions of people around the world, in lots of different languages, inspiring us all as we learn together about living passionately in our own unique ways. I am not exactly sure how this will happen, but will keep doing my best to get the word out.

Thank you, our reader, for your interest in our stories. I would love to hear how our journeys, lessons and reflections impact your life in positive ways!

Who am I and why do I matter?

I am a future Bestselling Author, joined by 21 future Bestselling Co-Authors, who are excited about inspiring people around the world to live passionately. I matter because I have put my whole heart into this project and feel fortunate to receive so much amazing support. I value my family and friends who have made this possible and who I am so blessed to spend joyful time with.

Who are you and why do you matter?

What are you so passionate about achieving that it hurts sometimes to even think about? Maybe you are afraid it won't work out? Consider how sad it might be if you never even try…

Maybe you don't know what you are passionate about yet and that is okay. You don't need to have the "final answer" now because, the truth is, there is no "final answer." Life is ever-changing. Try doing your daily routines in a different order and see how you feel. I invite you to muster some courage to explore some new options in your life. When you put yourself out of your comfort zone in simple activities, it prepares you for making life changes in a big way.

As you read each story in this book, notice which stories especially call you to explore new horizons in your life. You matter because there is no one exactly like you on this earth and you have something important to share with the world!

Tragedy to Empowerment: A Child's Loss Becomes Her Inspiration

Alison Orlando

Standing in front of the medicine cabinet with all of those bottles in front of me was overwhelming. I had no idea what I was looking for. All I knew was that my throat was sore, my cough was becoming a nuisance, and I hated being sick. At nine years old, I could not make out the names on all the bottles of medicine. I rummaged through the cabinet and yelled to my mom in the living room, "Mom, what do I take?" She quickly replied, "Second shelf down, the first bottle on the left." And there you have it. Moms know. And, thank goodness relief was on the way. What would I do without my mom? And I really meant that. What would I do without my mom?

Every young girl needs the guidance and love of her mother. She needs a mother's nurturing to gracefully grow into a confident young lady by following her mother's lead. I so desperately needed this. I so desperately longed for this. It was less than two weeks after I took that cough medicine that I lost my mom. She died in a car accident. I was lost and empty. Her passing opened a gaping wound in my heart that has taken all of my lifetime to heal.

How do you heal a young girl's heart that is so torn? Luckily, I was resilient; I put all my energy and focus into my schoolwork and sports. I excelled in all that I did and was recognized for that. As a young girl, I had everything I needed. I was a lucky, lucky girl, with a great home, great school, loving father, and a brother and sister who watched over me. But, my heart was broken and I felt lost. I wanted my mom, and good grades and a high batting average were not cutting it (not even close).

Independent, determined, demanding, tough, adventurous, and

loud are the adjectives my family provided when I asked them, "Words you would use to describe me as a kid?" I own these descriptions. These traits helped me get through lonely and challenging times through childhood. They also fostered my confidence to take care of myself and protect myself from being hurt (or at least I felt I needed to protect myself from being hurt). It was not the most graceful way to navigate childhood, but without a mom, I was coping the best way I knew how.

Suffering such a tragic loss and grieving so deeply helped me to understand this kind of suffering in other people. It was grueling for me and I would never want someone else to feel such pain. I learned, as a young adult, that helping others—even in small ways—was healing my heart little piece by little piece. This discovery led me to search for ways to help others suffering loss or hardship.

My college years afforded me many opportunities to volunteer. The community near Fordham University had much need and I felt I had much to give. I knew it would feel good to be involved in people's lives, but I didn't know I was to get so much more in return. I joined volunteer groups and donated my time. Tutoring and coaching grade school children, helping to build a home in White Plains, and volunteering at a hospice were some of the volunteer opportunities I took advantage of.

Searching for different ways to volunteer revealed opportunities to not just help those in my own backyard, but to travel to different places. I was a lucky, lucky teenager. I raised money to go overseas to volunteer my time and energy. I sent out letters to family and friends asking for donations and had endless bake sales. Each contributor who saw these causes as important played an integral part of my intention to help others and I am very grateful for that.

During my junior year of college, a small group of students traveled to Guatemala to build homes with Habitat for Humanity International. It was quite the workout, mixing the *mezcla* (cement) and laying bricks. Christmas break of my senior year (December 1995) was spent in Calcutta, India volunteering with the Missionaries of Charity. Mornings in Calcutta were spent at the Mother House for a breakfast of tea and a banana, and to celebrate Mass. Days were spent volunteering at Mother Teresa's Home for the Destitute and Dying and her Home for Abandoned Children.

There is a specific moment I recall that fueled my passion for helping and healing. I had a conversation with Mother Teresa during my stay in Calcutta. Mother Teresa was a small woman whose quiet words had grand meaning. She was also welcoming and witty. Mother Teresa made a lasting impression on me as she most likely did to everyone she met, even though, physically, she was so small you had to bend down to speak to her. When I greeted her, she took my hands in hers. Mother Teresa touched each of my fingers independently as she said the following words.

> *I will,*
> *I want,*
> *With God's*
> *Love*
> *To be holy.*
> *Feed me,*
> *Clothe me,*
> *Wash me,*
> *Care for me,*
> *Love me.*
> *Put them together and you are holy. It's that simple.*

Mother Teresa asked me, at that moment, if I would join the Missionaries of Charity. I was, well, a bit stunned. My response is quite funny in my opinion. I replied with a smile, "Thank you. I will think about it." She then reached into her pocket and handed me a small yellow card. Mother Teresa said, "Here, my business card." The card she handed me looked like this:

```
The fruit of SILENCE is Prayer
The fruit of PRAYER is Faith
The fruit of FAITH is Love
The fruit of LOVE is Service
The fruit of SERVICE is Peace
          Mother Teresa
```

It had been a long time since a mother figure had taken and held my hands, asked more of me than I ask of myself, and showed such care. It was a pinnacle moment of healing and growth for me. That young girl wishing to get over the loss of her mother was developing into a caretaker and helping to ease the loss of others. My passion was sparked and began to shine brightly.

I kept a journal during my stay in Calcutta; in this journal, I keep Mother Teresa's business card. The day we spoke, she wrote a message in my journal: "God Bless You." She kissed a Virgin Mary medallion and offered it to me. I shared a small intimate Mass with Mother Teresa each morning during my visit. Occasionally, I would see a photographer who would take a picture of her after the Mass. Mother Teresa said she had made a pact with God: God would allow one more person into heaven for each photograph taken of her.

Caring for a suffering woman and a motherless infant were experiences that opened my heart to the grace of unconditional love and care. Providing the human dignity a person deserves in her final moments and feeding a malnourished, abandoned infant are powerful, beautiful, and heartbreaking. Wait. Heartbreaking? Yes, more breaking of the heart, but all in an effort for my heart to repair and grow strong. I found joy in the sadness, and healing through the connections I made with those I touched. What began as a basic need for a little girl to heal her heart became a life-long passion. Through grieving the loss of my mother, I was learning to be a "mother" to others. Patching the wounds of others mended my heart and eased my loss.

My passion for helping culminated when I found myself in a career that allowed me to have it all. Yes, to have it all. I am currently able to help others and spend quality time with my family, enjoying the things that matter most. This career did not start out with a resume or an interview. It started from being unhappy, overweight, and not having the energy to keep up with my two young children. Not sounding like a typical career? Let me explain.

Having been a college athlete and active my whole life had made staying at a healthy weight a breeze. Having two children and reaching my mid-thirties changed that. I carried extra weight from the pregnancies and wasn't able to lose it. I was tired all the time. My weight yo-yoed for years. It brought me to a point of helplessness and disappointment. I was told by my doctor I needed to go on cholesterol medication—a scary prescription for a thirty-five-year-old. Not feeling great, and facing the possibility of having to go on a medication, I was ready for change.

I wanted my life back. I began a program called Take Shape For Life, and help was on its way. One of the best decisions of my life was to start that program. I had thought too hard and too long about my situation and never really knew how to help myself. I regained my health, body, and energy.

I lost weight, felt great, and did not need to go on any cholesterol medication. Taking control of my health was empowering and rewarding, but it got even better than that. I now help people to do the same thing I did; I became a health coach. Coaching people to achieve health and to reach their best has been an incredible means for me to reach and help so many. Taking my transformation full circle to now take part in other people's transformations is a passion, and—for me—the most fulfilling and rewarding lifework. I have collected the things that are most important to me and spark my passion—my family, our health, helping others, being surrounded by what matters most—and meshed them into a career.

Loving, loyal, committed, driven, fun-loving, fearless, having integrity, and loud—those are the adjectives my family provided when I asked them, "Words you would use to describe me as *adult*?" I am still loud, but have softened quite a bit from the little girl who assertively made her way through childhood, teen years, and young adulthood searching to be nurtured.

I am now a mom to two beautiful children and love caring for them and my husband. I am loved and taken care of by them, as well. I also care for the hundreds of clients I have coached. The successes of my clients and my family's love make me whole. And my healing continues. Serving on the board of a non-profit organization, the Andy K & Friends Charitable Foundation, allows me to help families suffering loss or hardship.

Passionate living is priceless, healing and rewarding. I feel like the luckiest woman. Don't ever let life's heartbreaks hinder you from finding your passion. Let your passion be contagious and watch it grow.

Alison's Lesson: Transforming Grief through Helping

Alison's story of transforming the grief resulting from her mother's tragic passing into a lifelong commitment to mothering many is absolutely beautiful. She was able to heal by giving what she was so dearly missing: the tender love of her mother. Alison is passionate about helping people and ready to assist with any cause she believes in, whether a charity, a new entrepreneur starting a business, or a person who wants to lose weight and live life. She has healed her grief through helping people with great love and built a successful business as well. I imagine Alison's mother and Mother Teresa are very proud of Alison!

Reflection

When tragedy strikes, taking time to grieve for this loss in your life is so important. There comes a time, however, when shedding more tears won't help. Instead of staying in this stuck and sad place, consider who might need *your* help. Who is suffering in a way you can relate to? How could you help someone—and yourself in the process—like Alison has, with humor and love?

PEACEFUL THUNDER:
SAY YES TO IT ALL. LIVING A
LIFE OF POWER, PEACE, AND JOY

Deborah Cohen

Pete Seeger died today.

I never met him, yet, in a way, he was a best friend. Pete personified my values. His were the songs I was raised on:

We Shall Overcome
Which Side Are You On?
If I Had a Hammer

I grew up singing these songs. Wide eyed, I listened to my parents' stories of fighting "Big Battles." They were union leaders, fought in WWII, and marched for equal rights. My father went into the Deep South to help Blacks organize to vote. I knew Fascists were bad. I heard and read about concentration camps. We discussed BIG ideas at our dining room table: socialism, communism, philosophy, art, theater, and science.

Who would I become in this story? Where would I make a difference? I dreamed of being Joan of Arc, or an Israeli Sabra, or perhaps discovering new radioactive elements like Marie Curie.

A bright and beautiful little girl, I sang with my father—we would harmonize. I took up folk dancing. I was an A student. The '60s hit and I fashioned myself a free spirit. Theater, chorus, year book, art squad . . . I was active in everything intellectual and creative. I went to rallies and marches for Vietnam, Kennedy, and Martin Luther King.

Integrity: Honoring Your Word

In our house, we knew that "all you had was your word;" you could lose everything, but to honor your word was the highest goal to live by. Danny was my baby brother. I loved Danny and instinctively knew I was supposed to take care of him. I was about seven and he was five when a huge snowstorm struck as we were coming home from school. We walked home from school in those days (the 1950s). Mom worked and she had set up a deal with a local luncheonette so that we were fed hamburgers and French fries while we would wait for her to get home. That day, in the blizzard, the luncheonette was closed. I knew what to do. We would go to a neighbor's house. Yes. My friend Joanne's mom was usually home. We knocked on the door and I remember vividly looking up at Joanne's mother in her housecoat and curlers as she said "You can come in, but I cannot have a boy stay here with my daughter. Your brother will have to go somewhere else."

In that frightening moment, I made a decision. I listened to my elder, did what I was told, and went in to the house. Danny, at just five years old, plodded on through the blizzard to the Rabbi's house three blocks away. My mother, driving home from work, didn't know where we were. (Obviously, there were no cell phones in 1957.) She saw her little boy trudging through the snow. I heard that story over and over for many years, with my mother's shocked "and she sent him out into the snow. A little boy."

I knew the fault was really mine. I had never told anyone that I was supposed to take care of Danny, but I knew that was my responsibility. It was my word, my promise . . . and I had failed. What had I done? I had listened to an authority, even though I knew what she was saying wasn't right. I would never do that again. Where had I gone wrong? I realize, now, that I didn't really have the courage to stand for my convictions.

Here Is My First Challenge: Integrity

How would I make up for being weak? In that moment I told myself that I would be known as a "good girl": responsible and reliable. These are two traits I am known for. And . . . there has also been the side that rejected authority and broke the rules. The part that became a hippie and lived outside the norm. The side that never married, that fought for great ideals, women's rights, free speech, and free love.

My challenge—and what SPARKS my passion—is to dance between the opposites created by a seven-year-old. Either dutifully being a good girl, responsible and reliable, or being wild, creative, and irresponsible. I became a caregiver, midwife, nurse, and life coach. I led rituals for hundreds with wild drumming and dancing. I studied and became adept as an alternative healer. I have, in my sixties, melded these worlds, walking in a "crooked straight line on the path to God." I learned to love every step and misstep that got me here.

And what about my little brother? Dan died suddenly, unexpectedly, just two years ago. Thank you, precious brother. I am sorry I let you down. I love you.

Courage: Making a Difference

I am looking at a photo album. There are many photos of my parents in May Day labor parades in New York City. In the first one, they are wheeling a stroller with me in it, next to us is a young Black couple, with their little baby. This was 1952. I am so proud that my parents took that stand. I knew I was also born to make a difference.

Mom worked full time, teaching first grade. We had a woman who helped clean. I would play with her child, usually in the yard. We were six years old. They were black. We were white. I don't think I realized that at the time—the difference.

I remember, one day, my mother calling to me to come quickly. She and I hid behind the door as my father answered it. There were four or five men, all men I knew as neighbors and fathers of my friends. They were carrying shovels and rakes, just like they had been working in their yards . . . but somehow it was ominous. My dad listened to them say that they didn't want me and the "little black child" playing in the front yard where their children could see. He told them it was a free country and that I would play with my friend. I was very young, yet I was SO proud of my father. And, I was frightened. Later, when I learned about the Nazis and the Ku Klux Klan, I understood what was really happening that day.

Later, in college, I marched in an anti-Vietnam rally. I remember my dad telling me to be careful, and not to have my photograph taken. He reminded me of the McCarthy period, when he and his friends had been blacklisted and some others had been deported. I grew up hearing about his and my mother's heroism during the war, and on the picket lines back home. And, once, he even had to be hidden in the trunk of a car in the Deep South to escape the police tracking dogs looking for those northern organizers helping Blacks to register to vote.

Here Is a Second Challenge: Courage

How willing could I be to stand for what I believe? I became a lay midwife, helping women to birth their babies naturally, with dignity, in their own homes. I marched on the front lines against Viet Nam. I have taken a stand for the purity of our food, water, and air, for people to live with dignity, and for a living wage, for children to be protected from harm. I have coached hundreds to step out of their boxes, to be free and take the actions they might fear.

This challenge has taken on many layers. I watch as my ninety-five-year-old mom continues to be involved in social action, making a difference in her community, raising funds to help those who cannot help themselves find health and wellbeing. I have the honor of having a partner who has chosen the difficult path of standing for social justice. The challenge is knowing when to lay down the sword and shield, and when to pick it up. It is another dance in living life fully.

The Third Challenge: Freedom

I was SO excited to be in college, and to have the freedom to live the way I believed. I signed up for a coed dormitory. I immediately joined a group protesting the Viet Nam war. There was a beautiful professor talking about our rights. Long hair down his back. So intelligent, so stirring. We had an affair. He said "no problem," he had an open marriage. It was, he didn't. I naively didn't see the drinking. He separated from his wife and I got pregnant. I look back and see more clearly now an eighteen-year-old starry-eyed little girl and a thirty-three-year-old university professor.

How can one be free to live one's life AND take care of other's needs? We had children. My challenge was to balance being responsible to myself . . . to our children . . . and to their father.

In many ways, that stage of my life was amazing. My man was brilliant, and often in our living room we had scientists and philosophers. We discussed ideas and concepts. I learned more than I would have in a graduate degree. (Thank you, Jon, for an incredible education.) But, when drinking, Jon was emotionally abusive, and for many reasons, it soon became clear that our time together would have to end. My challenge was to have my leaving work for everyone. For Jon, for his new love Leslie, and for their children. For me to be free and make the difference I wanted to make. I took a stand that we would all be friends, parent the children together, and make family decisions together. My goal was that my children would have a family . . . and I would have the time to pursue my education and goals.

We did it. To this day, we are all friends. We visit each other's homes and spend big family holidays together. When the children were in school, at parent/teacher day they would introduce us: "This is my dad, this is my mom, and this is my other mother."

Challenges morph and take on new forms. Inside the challenge of freedom, when I left Jon, I never again trusted a man with my life. I had many passionate, warm, loving, sexy relationships—and I am still in contact with—and friends with—most of them. Yet, I never married. I "knew" that, in marriage, a woman loses her freedom. I structured my life to be free. And, I loved it.

My challenge today is to be free *inside* a relationship. Ah. Quite a dance. Today, I have chosen to live with a wonderful man. He is kind, good, and loving. I am learning to trust in his love and caring. It SPARKS my passion, at sixty-four, to explore the steps of a new dance. I am finding the capacity to be compassionate while sharing this deep intimacy. How much will I retreat to the familiar wonderful place of being alone—or open my heart, be soft, and see the sacredness of another's gentle heart? This is a daily practice and challenge. Life doesn't get much better than embracing a challenge.

I have learned there is no secret. It's all a balancing act of opposites. The trick is to stay open, fluid, willing to change and willing to greet the dark.

Pete Seeger died today.

What song will I sing now?

My song and my business name is *Peaceful Thunder*. The art of being powerful AND peaceful. Yes, it is in the dance of our contradictions that we creatively design our lives. My joy is to support others in having it all. My clients find their passion and design their own song to experience the miracle of a life well lived.

Deborah's Lesson: Flowing with Life

Deborah shares her three challenges, living with:

- Integrity
- Courage
- Freedom

Through each adventure that Deborah faced from her childhood through adulthood, she has taken time to reflect, to face the darkness, in order to find the light. She honors her passions while honoring the people that she loves and cares for. The wisdom that she has gained through her life and careers inspires her clients to, "find their passion and design their own song to experience the miracle of a life well lived." I know that Deborah does this well, since I have received inspiring coaching from her.

Reflection

I imagine that you sometimes feel stuck and unsure of how to proceed in creating your passionate life, just as I have. Have you ever worked with a coach to help you see situations from a new perspective?

THE RX DIARIES: RECOVERY, REBIRTH & RELEASE FROM ADDICTION

Wendy Blanchard, M.S.

From the minute I went into treatment for prescription drug addiction, mental health issues, and eating disorders, I decided that I was going to tell my story truthfully, and leave no stone unturned. I have been successful in carrying out that goal, and it has been empowering. I talk a lot about my addiction, and mental health challenges, and the fact that I now realize that I have been suffering with a variety of mental health challenges, and eating disorders, since I was a teen. Each day, as I gain more clarity, I am able to understand the depth of my co-occurring disorders, and how they have affected my life, and the lives of everyone around me. I believe that these disorders began early on in my life, due to the complex childhood trauma—and subsequent adolescent and adult traumas—that I suffered. Unfortunately, I never received the help that I needed over the years, until recently, and it remains an ongoing process.

At age fourteen, when I began using codeine sulfate to numb real physical pain, I quickly learned how I could numb the deep emotional pain that I was suffering from, which nobody around me seemed to acknowledge. Over the past decade or so, I began to feel that I was disconnected, which ultimately ended in a complete break from reality. It's the addiction in concert with co-occurring disorders that causes the disconnect in our brains, literally. Addiction and mental illness are real brain diseases, and they are devastating, progressive diseases if left untreated. Fortunately, they can be arrested, treated, and managed, but "it takes a village"—a loving, supportive, caring, beautiful village—that I have been so blessed to call my own.

I never felt good enough, pretty enough, or smart enough at anything in my life. I am not going to place blame on anyone else because that will not change my past, nor will it help me to heal. I WILL NOT allow my addiction, or mental health challenges, to define who I am any longer. I KNOW who I am now, and I am so proud of the hard work that I have done since I have been in recovery. I truly believe in myself, and I know that I am on the cusp of accomplishing a great deal for myself, my children, my granddaughter, and people worldwide, in the field of mental health, addiction, and wellness.

I will no longer hide behind a mask trying to be someone who I am not. I'm a pretty perfect version of who I am, and with the support team that I have—and the loving support of my family, friends, and community—I will continue to progress and achieve my dreams. I am in addiction/mental health recovery, and I will not be ashamed of that, or apologize for it, any longer. Both of these are real diseases that need to be researched, treated, managed, and discussed with love, understanding, compassion, kindness, courage, guidance, and support. I am being given the opportunity to raise awareness, and to educate and empower others about these diseases through my businesses, The Rx Diaries and Blissfully Gl-Airy Free, LLC, and my weekly radio show, *The Rx Diaries*. I hope to continue to help many people who are suffering, struggling, and feeling lost, scared, and disconnected, just the way that I have done throughout my life.

Right before I went into treatment, on April 3, 2013, I was broken, scared, and alone, and there was nobody there to comfort me, or to help me. I will do everything that I can, using every resource that I have, to reach out, and to help as many others as I can. I will make sure that I am there to comfort, help, guide, support, and love them through their own addiction and mental health recovery. These diseases are misunderstood, misdiagnosed, and—in my opinion—sometimes mismanaged.

I have learned that practicing holistic, organic, and natural means of healing gets to the root of many illnesses of the body, mind, and spirit. Ongoing learning and practicing leads to a whole healthy lifestyle. I have been practicing a clean and green, gluten-free, dairy-free, sugar-free, grain-free lifestyle, and nourishing my body with natural, organic foods.

I have also been practicing spirituality, exercise, and Yoga, and have received energy healing, essential oil treatments, the Emotional Freedom Technique, and Raindrop Therapy, just to name a few, which have helped me tremendously. Life coaching, Holistic Health Coaching, Functional medicine, psychotherapy, and a twelve-step program, also to name a few, have been powerful catalysts in re-connecting me to society. Throughout my recovery, I am learning so much about myself. I am learning to truly love myself, and others; accept myself and others; respect myself, and others; and enjoy being with myself, and others. I am learning how to be a present, engaged, happy, independent, and successful human being both personally and professionally. I am able to think outside the box, and to leave my comfort zone. I am able to embrace life as I search further for answers in my spirituality, as well as my personal and professional life. I am proud of my businesses, The Rx Diaries and Blissfully Gl-Airy Free, LLC, and my weekly radio show, *The Rx Diaries*.

Wendy's Lesson: Transforming from Addiction to Empowerment

Wendy experienced a tremendous amount of trauma in her life, starting at a young age, and did not have adults to support and teach her other ways, she did the best that she could with what she had.

I met Wendy shortly after her discharge from rehabilitation, when she was eager to learn about herself, and how to connect with people in healthy ways. Wendy's newfound zest for life was—and still is—inspiring. Her dedication to helping not only herself, but many people, recover from addiction in holistic ways will bring deep and lasting healing. Wendy is sharing her experiences with addiction and recovery in order to help people suffering from addiction, which is an epidemic in this country. I admire Wendy's courage to share her story. Wendy is extremely honest and willing to put ideas into action. She notices what works for her, and what does not work for her, which is an important distinction. We are all unique and need to experiment to find what works best for us individually.

Through her business, The Rx Diaries, Wendy is guiding people to resources that help individuals and their loved ones to heal, and she also has an ongoing dialogue about addiction and mental illness through her radio show, *The Rx Diaries* on IntentionRadio.com. Wendy has been empowered by sharing her inspiring story, and—leading by example—she is helping many people to heal from addiction.

Reflection

A key tool for healing in general—which also applies to addiction—is learning how to process emotions in a healthy way. When emotions are not acknowledged, or are ignored or disregarded, they become trapped in our body, causing disease in many forms. The SPARKS Inspiration cards and classes help people to process emotions in a healthy way.

A valuable skill that takes courage and practice is learning to feel emotions as they come through our body, and noticing what messages are being delivered. Too often, people will numb their feelings because, let's be honest here, strong feelings can be scary. Emotions are a tool to help us understand what is happening, what is working, and what is not working in our lives.

For example, anger is an emotion that too many, especially women, are taught not to express. So anger gets buried, building resentment and guilt inside, which leads to heartache and disease. When anger visits me, it is a message that my emotional or physical safety is being invaded and protection is needed. I know now, after lots of practice, that I need to take time to discern where this emotion is coming from. I ask myself whether it is coming from a present situation, a past memory, or a trapped emotion. (You will read more about trapped emotions in future chapters.)

Has addiction or mental illness touched your life in some way? Try beginning, as Wendy did, by speaking the truth about what is happening. Seek help from friends, professionals, and holistic practitioners who will guide you and your loved ones to find healing and healthy alternatives. Would embracing yourself and your life with the zest and positivity that Wendy exudes help you to overcome challenges in your life? Let us look at this SPARKS Inspiration Courage card as an example of how to handle fears in a healthy manner:

Courage!

When I have waited a long time to address my fears, they seem SO BIG!

I need to slow down and address one issue at a time.

Healing:

I create a worry list and then prioritize what should be handled first, second, third.

Affirmation:

I feel the power of knowing that challenges are solved courageously, one step at a time.

~ Maria Blon & Ann Bell

LIVING FULLY, EVEN WHEN CAREGIVING

Sue Keane

My greatest challenge in life was raising my son Evan. Evan has profound developmental delays since he functions at the level of a 3 month old baby, has cerebral palsy and a severe seizure disorder, is in a wheelchair, and is dependent on others for everything in his life.

After having two healthy children, Maria and Paul, I was looking forward to raising Evan and expected that he would be similar to my other children. Evan was born a beautiful, blue-eyed, handsome baby who was "normal" the first few months, rolling over and pushing himself up with his arms. When he was around three months old, he started losing these skills and his development reversed. These beginning times when we didn't know what was wrong with Evan were very worrying. I became depressed and didn't feel like eating. I woke up very early, around 2:00 or 3:00 am, and couldn't go back to sleep.

When Evan was a few months old, he started having seizures. The pediatrician sent him to the ER, saying they would admit him for a complete work-up. He was there for a week. No specific cause was found; Evan's brain was just not hooked up correctly. The first few years were very tough, as we were working out the best combination of seizure medications—many of which made him sleepy.

We traveled to Australia, when he was two, to visit my parents. He wound up in Children's Hospital in Melbourne three times with severe seizure problems. After six weeks, we made it home. We faced many more hospital visits over the years. Now, at thirty-two, Evan takes four different seizure meds that give him quite good control over his seizures, although he is often sleepy. He hasn't been in the hospital or gone to the ER in five years, which is amazing.

Also when Evan was two, he went to an Easter Seal school one mile from our house for five years. We got great support from the staff and therapists, and it was very helpful getting to know parents facing similar difficulties. For example, the children were all developmentally delayed to different degrees, and some had cerebral palsy or delayed development.

Since Evan was attending school five days a week, I had the opportunity to start a new career. In five years, I earned an associate degree in accounting. I really enjoyed going back to school, because I could focus on something other than Evan's challenges. After that, I took the H&R Block basic tax prep course and worked for them for nine years, working while Evan was at school. Working was very enjoyable for me and I learned skills that I will use for the rest of my life. I was no longer depressed, and felt I could handle Evan's many problems with my family's help. I now volunteer, doing taxes in low-income areas. I enjoy volunteering, because I can use my skills to help other people who cannot afford to have professional help.

One of my passions is being physically active. My husband Bill and I continued to play tennis, swim, hike, and bike even after Evan was born. We found ways to include him whenever possible. He was often in the racquet club nursery while Bill and I went swimming or played tennis. One day, a woman came up to me in the locker room asking if I was Evan's mother. She said her son used to read to Evan when he was there with him and said Evan really enjoyed it. Other children also seemed to enjoy Evan. I used a baby sitter who had a day care service in her house. She told me that, when Evan was there at naptime, the kids always wanted to nap in the room with Evan. In many ways, Evan was a blessing not only for us but to many people.

Bill and I were fortunate to have good doctors for Evan and we met some amazing, good people while caring for him. He went everywhere with us, riding in his special needs Baby Jogger as we walked on the beach in Cape Cod. We often had the early dinner special at the Grand Concourse Restaurant. We would sit near the piano because, when Evan was alert and doing well, he would sing "Ah-ah-ah" on and on and the piano would drown out the noise a bit, so that he would not bother the other diners. In the summer, I would put Evan in the baby pool outside when it had warmed up from the sun. He just floated with a life jacket and seemed very relaxed.

Bill and I had Evan at home until he was fourteen, when it became very difficult physically to care for him. He now resides at Allegheny Valley School, an intensive care facility, helping people with developmental disabilities to reach their fullest potential. Evan receives wonderful care, with physical, occupational, and speech therapy and is able to continue swimming with a life jacket in a pool heated to ninety-two degrees. I usually see him once a week to feed him dinner and, when we can, go outside into the lovely garden.

What I learned from raising Evan is that it is important to seek support, which we received from our family, friends, and professionals. Raising Evan was a challenge but a great pleasure due to his pleasant personality. He has brought joy to my life and the lives of many others who have encountered him. As the supervisor on his floor at the Allegheny Valley School said: "Evan is from Heaven," and I couldn't agree more.

Sue's Lesson: Solve the Problem and Have Fun

My mother Sue has handled the challenges in her life with determination and a sense of adventure. She and my father Bill, while in their seventies, were the oldest white-water paddlers on the rivers near Pittsburgh, Pennsylvania many times. Whenever challenges arrive in Sue's life, she assesses the situation and starts working on solutions right away, seeking support when she needs it. Purchasing the baby jogger allowed Sue and Bill to continue hiking and spending time in nature, which was also good for Evan. Notice how Sue started a new career, which helped her to focus on something other than her worries.

As I reflect on how Sue managed caring for Evan so graciously, I have a hunch that a lot of her success had to do with continuing to exercise and enjoy life.

Reflection

When life-changing challenges come into your life, taking time to assess the situation and the changes that will need to take place are the first priorities. Often, caregivers put their own needs last—which may be necessary at times—but if this practice is continued too long it can cause problems for everyone involved.

How balanced is your life in terms of taking care of your family and friends in relation to taking time for yourself? How active are you? Do you get outside in nature and exercise no matter what challenges you face? Make a commitment to go on adventures and have fun. You will be helping yourself and the people you care for!

Living to the Beat of Her Own Drum

Carina Blon

At the young age of twenty-one, Carina has done more to help people than many have done in an entire lifetime, and she is not finished. I find her story one of great inspiration. I feel so honored that Carina is my daughter. I want her story to be shared around the world in order to inspire people to follow their dreams and their heart. I hope that Carina will write her own memoirs when she is ready, but, for this book, she has graciously given me permission to use her blog posts for this book. I've narrated my views in between.

Carina has a zest for life. When she was little, her favorite color was fuchsia. She loved to have bright outfits that she created, to play dress up, dance, sing, paint, and to organize her friends in plays and other games. She loved snow, playing outside for hours in her fuchsia snowsuit with her friends. Carina changed as she became a teen. Her hair became curly though it had been straight, earth tones rather than fuchsia dominated her wardrobe, and she felt sad to let go of being young and carefree. Carina wanted to do something meaningful in her life, which included helping in a third world country. While Carina did well in high school, many classes seemed pointless to her. In fact, one night, Carina had a panic attack so severe that she and I were in the emergency room in the middle of the night. She was having trouble breathing and her heart was racing. Why? Carina couldn't decide on what to study in college. Tom and I never pushed her into applying for colleges because she didn't seem ready, but since most of her friends were going away to school, she felt a lot of pressure. A few months after that scary night in the hospital, Carina and I were on our way to Haiti after the earthquake, a story that you were introduced to in my chapter. Carina found her passion in Haiti, amazed and inspired me. I imagine her story opening many people's eyes to new possibilities for discovering their careers.

Carina handled Haiti so much better than I, staying calm and focusing on the positive possibilities that arose throughout our days there. She loved the people, and they loved her. The children (wearing varying amounts of clothes and shoes) would follow Carina down the street all singing the world cup soccer theme song, "Waka Waka" and "Wavin' Flag". When we visited Shad's cousin's school, which had been damaged by the earthquake, we adults were looking around, wondering what to do. Carina, at seventeen years old, said, "Let's knock the school down and clean it up." We followed Carina's lead and soon children and adults were pitching in to help us. Through the generosity and hard work of many people, the school re-opened in October 2010. Carina's Christmas present that year was to spend the week in Haiti. She saved the money she made working as a lifeguard, and flew to Haiti for her spring break, as well.

Carina graduated from high school in June 2011. In July 2011, Carina bought a one-way ticket to Haiti, and moved there. Carina knew that she wanted to get to know the people in Haiti—especially the children at the school we helped start and their families. Beyond that, Carina did not know how she would be helping.

Following are Carina's blog posts, describing just a few of her experiences.

Harsh realities

In June 2011, Jean Elie Cadet, a student at the school, died due to complications of malnutrition. It was a tragedy to lose this sweet little boy, who was generous to a fault. This is Carina's blog post after hearing of Jean Elie's passing.

Numb. I just felt numb. Because I just couldn't believe. Couldn't conceive, that our beautiful caring little guy, Jean Elie, would never draw more pictures with half crayons. Would never go into second grade, and could never be a psychologist. Never eat another spaghetti and sauce with his classmates, never look to me with his super sweet eyes, never hide another granola bar from school in his book bag to bring home to his struggling family. Which was amazing to consider. How supremely unselfish and impressive, but most of all heartbreaking and painful to witness a four-year-old child save his only snack of the day to bring home to his brothers and sisters and parents.

Seeing this act once or twice, I never knew the seriousness of his family's situation, and I wish with all that is in me that we could have found out another way besides a funeral.

I know this has shown me that the small details must be paid attention to, that families must have adequate food above everything else, and that, for me, I need to live and work towards never allowing this to happen to another sweet, caring, unselfish, innocent young child ever again.

After Jean Elie's tragic death, money was raised to feed the children twice a day with the help of parents who volunteered to cook. Many common happenings in Haiti are unfathomable to anyone who has never visited a third world country.

Here are Carina's thoughts on "homes" in Haiti.

A Home?

The cooking fire filled the makeshift tent with a warm glow and thick smoke, a contrast to the outside world of steady rain and cool air. Small children huddled; where the water didn't drip, they were sleeping. Was it the smoke or emotion that stung my eyes with tears falling like the rains from tropical storms?

Muddy, uneven dirt ground, nails in bottle caps in tree branch beams and scraps of corrugated metal and tarps make a home, rain water leaking in drips, a wise-tough-strong motherly face on a tired body, tattered clothes and scraps, branches in a heap for the cooking fire, floured fish and vegetables ready for market the next day, small children seemingly sleeping on a sheet of cardboard placed on top of cinder blocks while a steady rain pours outside.

Haiti is a Caribbean country, sharing the island of Hispaniola with the Dominican Republic to the east. The capital city is Port au Prince and the official languages are Haitian Creole and French. There are an estimated 9 million inhabitants, and the country is known as the poorest economically in the Western hemisphere. On January 12, 2010, a magnitude 7.0 earthquake struck near the capital city, leaving countless people dead, injured, and homeless.

How is this fair? In this world of space travel, economically friendly building permits, million-dollar wedding cakes, and ten-year-olds with iPads, how are there still people without a home? Tears cannot solve anything and the rain doesn't help a tent camp either. Those children came to her tent because theirs was leaking worse. Barefoot, we decided to carry those children to the house and they slept on an air mattress that night and other rainy nights that followed. The rain made small rivers and streams and caked mud on everything in the morning. Later, some people planted gardens when others left the camp, but then it seemed the rain didn't fall as much. An NGO offered a relocation program for the masses, little by little people left this nest. Where once almost 300 bodies bustled, now the land is silent, sleeping below the cinder block walls and foundations beginning to rise.

Within five months of moving to Haiti, Carina was fluent in Creole, the language of the common people. She learned mostly from spending time with the moms when they were cooking, and by working with the children. At first, Shad was worried about how people would treat Carina and was strict about asking her not to go out in the streets on her own. Over time, Shad relaxed as people got to know and trust Carina.

When visitors came, Carina would take them to visit the children's homes. She made a map of where all the children at the school lived and also wrote a profile for each child at the school with a picture and description of their family. Carina was quite the celebrity. People would call, "Carina" wherever she walked. Here is a blog post about a woman she met on her travels.

"I was just sitting too much"

As I was standing on the river bank waiting for "the boys"—a group of them who are always there to help clean or carry things and provide some security—to finish swimming and jumping in the river, someone from across the river was calling me. I definitely could not make out who it was but as she got closer, I could see that she was balancing a big tray on her head, and I saw she was one of the girls that we've visited in the tent camp. I haven't visited her in a while, and it was really nice to see her. I asked her what started her selling and she said "I was just sitting too much." Whenever I used to see her in the tent camp, she was always sitting, with her 5-month-old baby or her friend looking kind of sad and a bit lo.st Seeing her today, she looked really strong, free and happy.

Gardening Brings= Hope

Carina started gardens on the roof where she lived with Shad, Danielo, and Wildo. Danielo enjoyed helping Carina grow fruits, vegetables, and flowers.

Carina also started a compost pile at home and beautiful gardens at the school. Here are a few short blogs Carina wrote about the environment, gardening and creating a map.

Last week, we visited a nursery. All types of fruit trees, flowering trees, shrubs, plants, and seedlings everywhere. All people read of Haiti's environment is the deforestation, but there are a lot of beautiful lush areas.

There were about 11 cans of formula in storage that [were] expired. So I emptied out the powder, and planted tomato and sweet pepper plants. Planning to give them to families on house visits.

We have painted a map of Haiti on the wall inside. Wildo really took a lead on this and did a lot of tracing, painting, and wrote all of the department and city names.

Carina wanted to find ways to help the students' parents earn money by learning what their talents were. She helped start an animal livestock program, a women's sewing and craft circle, and a women's health circle.

Going to Jecelene's house today made my day. They have a new goat from the animal program and she said it's going to be her best friend. Her mom and she are so funny together; they're spunky and full of energy all the time. Jecelene's mom is Veronique and she makes beautiful jewelry and these belts with hemp that the volunteers donated. We are trying to get a good business setup going for her to sell them and make good profits.

Musings on Economy

There's giving a man a fish, and teaching a man to fish... How about building fish ponds?

Yesterday morning, I brought a can of tuna fish that was lying around, across the street for Elcie's cat to eat. Elcie owns a small store and she sells literally everything you need in a day. Her cat is really skinny and, as we were sitting there watching her gobble up the meat, I asked Elcie what would happen if we gave the cat a can of tuna every day. She said the little cat would get used to eating the free tuna and not meow or be interested in scaring away any mice or rats that sometimes crawl into the shelves. Which led me to think... What if this situation was applied to her customers? If someone gives each of Elcie's clients an ingredient or food or product they use the most, what would happen to her business?

What would happen to her five daughters, all in high school and college, which their mom pays for?

And the merchants that sell her toys, bread, razors, condoms, crazy glue, rum, kids' toys, cooking ingredients, charcoal, baked goods, drinks, OTC medicines, baby food, ice, mosquito repellent, light bulbs, batteries, bleach, soap, hair products, and school supplies?

And the merchants and factories that supply those merchants with supplies?

And what would happen to the people giving out that one ingredient to each of her costumers? Could they run out of ingredients?

What happens, then, when the customers don't have their ingredients anymore? Will Elcie's business still be there? If she is, will she still have the ingredients after a long time of no one buying them?

Today I expressed these questions to her, kind of jokingly and hy-

pothetically, and we laughed. A few kids outside her store said things like "Yeah, why don't more people just give us money?"

Puzzles

Yesterday, I was in the kitchen helping to clean dishes and one of the kids who was around had pieces of this puzzle with parts of fish and deep sea plants in his pocket. It must have a million pieces, because I see them around everywhere—near the bookshelves, scattered near the garbage can overflowing with empty water bags and coconut shells, on the porch with benches for the kids, even in the walkway and street outside. Anyway, I sat down and tried to help him match a few pieces, and a couple other kids gathered around. Clearly their technique was a bit different than mine, as they would pick up two pieces and jam them together to make them fit as I tried to find a match of two somewhere. I tried explaining that some just don't work, they don't go together . . . but then it hit me that this is Haiti. We make things fit.

The sifter the guys used to make the concrete the past few days was part of an old fan, the knife our moms use to cut the white part of coconuts, lemons, and meat is also used to pull weeds out of our garden, and open the bulk bags of rice, brown sugar, and beans for the kids. Right now, in this internet place, there are no electrical outlets and there are cords that run across the ceiling and the open wires are wrapped around the cord that powers these five laptops. I have even seen the same orange t-shirt on a 12-year-old kid, a middle-aged man and an elderly, pretty large woman, here.

So maybe that puzzle will never be a picture of the ocean floor, because the pieces are everywhere. But really it's good to see these "mismatched together" pieces. We see it's a puzzle, so why shouldn't all the pieces have a fit? They look pretty cool, and it would be a neat art project to paint or glue them together, for magnets or sculptures or picture frames or maybe buttons on a play spaceship we could make.

Teaching?

I have been in Haiti volunteering for a school for almost two years. I am mostly in the office, on the laptop, contacting supporters, updating our facebook page and website, and researching cool project ideas for the teachers. I also take care of the supply closet and prize bin, setting up skype sessions between our school and classes in NY and also this year I tried to do some English lessons for our students in preschool to second grade.

I like being with the school—working for the teachers and students, and being the bridge between supporters in the US and our staff and community here. It is hard work but also rewarding, and I like to think I am making a difference. I strive to pay attention to what the parents of our students want, and last school year the parents had expressed an interest in their kids learning English. So I thought I should make time to do thirty-minute English classes a few times a week for each of the four classes. I tried reading children's picture books, teaching songs, counting, the alphabet, but . . . .As it turns out, I don't have the patience to be a teacher, especially for these young, sweet but full of energy—kids. I couldn't get them to sit down, to stop talking or fighting with each other, singing other songs, or coming up to sit on my lap or play with my hair. One week, I made a PowerPoint presentation of what the state of New York is like. I had pictures of the city tall buildings, the Statue of Liberty, traffic, subways, the Empire State Building. I included poems that one of the classes in our partner schools in NYC had written about a subway and a food market. I had pictures of the suburbs with houses, neighborhoods, school buses and parks. I had slides of the urban areas- the Adirondacks, mountains, cabins, and big lakes. Then the four seasons, and I collected pictures from my childhood: my family in the snow, my friends sledding in the winter, and carving jack-o'-lanterns in the fall, and at the beach in the summer.

So, I decided to show the PowerPoint to our second graders—the oldest students of the school. Their teacher is really smart and is a great teacher, and most of the time they are very well behaved with her, so I thought it wouldn't be a problem to show them this PowerPoint that I thought they would be totally interested in. For the first two minutes, their teacher was in the room and they paid attention when she showed them where New York is on the map. Then I started to show them pictures of New York City, and they were fine. When their teacher left, Bertha pinched Sherlanda, so Sherlanda yelled to me that Bertha pinched her. Luckenson asked me when he could go to visit New York and someone asked what the buildings are made of. [Good questions, but they didn't raise their hands. Luckenson's *question also broke my heart, because the chance of most Haitians getting to live or visit another country is very slim.] Danielo switched his seat and Roodler didn't want to sit next to him, and then Wisguens went to sit next to Danielo, too. But Wisguens stepped on Martide's toe and she screamed at him. So I tried to continue to present the PowerPoint, showing the Statue of Liberty, a bird's-eye view from the Empire State Building, city traffic intersections, and, finally, trying to translate the poems. I think some of the students heard some of the poem, but most of them weren't really paying attention. So, in the middle of the poem, I just told them all [that] they could go back to class because I couldn't talk over them. Protests, and then I said "No, we are finished today, and another day when Ms. Louna [their teacher] says the class will be well behaved, [you] can come back to see the rest of the presentation."*

So that day I was pretty discouraged. I realized I didn't have the education or patience to be a teacher—and I don't want to be a teacher. It wasn't that great a day after that, because it was kind of the last straw for my teaching attempts, and I mostly wrote emails and worked on the website page for the organization. The next day was school again and I came back with a fresh mind, but I knew I didn't want to do a classroom again. I sent some emails, helped the teachers get their supplies, organized shelves, gave out prizes to students the teachers sent to me, and spent some time in the cafeteria. Then, right after school ended at one o'clock, Luckenson, one of the second graders, came into the office with a beautiful drawing of the Statue of Liberty, which I had shown his class from the PowerPoint. I was pretty happy. I gave him a prize from the prize box and I had him sit in my chair and took a picture for the school Facebook page. I told him "Mesi Anpil," which means "Thank you Very much," and we both were all smiles. It just made my day that he had remembered and wanted to draw the Statue of Liberty. And it made me have hope that I could show the class the rest of the PowerPoint and there would be someone who will learn something or remember it. I think it was the next day that Ms. Louna gave the ok for her students to come and watch the rest of the "Life in New York" presentation. The students were better behaved and I was calmer, knowing that even if one of the students learned something, the work would have been worth it.

Carina called me in the fall of 2013, excited that teaching the children that year was going so much better. In December of 2013, Carina became very sick with typhoid fever and malaria. She had a wonderful doctor in Haiti, and Dr. Lynch (her pediatrician) kept in contact to make sure that the treatments were complete. Carina did recover, but the experience was really nerve-wracking for all of us. Although we were scheduled to visit in less than a month, many times I thought of flying down to Haiti before our scheduled flight or having Carina fly back here. But she had all she needed in Haiti: medicine and people who took care of her. Shad hired a woman named Alourde to cook and clean for them, which is something that they should have done long before.

Life in Haiti is hard. Food is cooked on a fire or over charcoal, and clothes are washed by hand. There is dust everywhere, so things get dirty fast. When Tom and I arrived in Haiti on New Year's Eve, Carina was relieved to have us there. She was ready to return to the States, but needed our support. Deciding to leave was heart-wrenching, but the right decision for her at the time. The teachers at the school were encouraging to Carina, pointing out the importance of taking time to get her education. The amount of love and respect the teachers have for Carina is beautiful. They compared Carina to Jesus, because she came to live as they did, not as an outsider.

This is just a sneak peek of the thoughts and experiences of Carina over her two and a half years of volunteering and living in Haiti. I look forward to someday reading her memoirs as they will be rich and deep with her love for the people in Haiti.

Carina's Lesson: Giving by Observing and Listening

Carina helped a community of people by observing how they interact and live their lives on a day-to-day basis. She listened to what was important to them before making suggestions. How beautiful that she honored the Haitian people and their culture by getting to know them well, and, in turn, Carina was embraced by her Haitian community.

I feel so much pride for all that she has done and, quite frankly, relieved that she is now back in the States, healthy. Beginning her career by volunteering gave her a strong foundation of real practical learning, which she can draw upon to enhance her college education, career, and life. Unlike when she was in high school, Carina loves her college classes in community and human services administration, because she knows how valuable education is from experience. This quote by Mother Theresa exemplifies the spirit with which Carina has helped the people in Haiti:

> *Love is not patronizing and charity isn't about pity, it is about love. Charity and love are the same—with charity you give love, so don't just give money but reach out your hand instead. ~ Mother Teresa*

Reflection

Parents, I urge you to listen to your children and honor their interests. Too often, children and teens are encouraged to go to school and head to college even if they have no idea what they want to study. Time and money are wasted as teens follow someone else's idea of how to live life. How interesting life would be if we all followed the beat of our own drum, just as Carina has. Imagine if we took more time to observe each other, to listen more and talk less. What hidden talents and interests would grow and bloom?

Is there something that you have always wanted to try? Start planning and follow your dreams. You never know where your ideas will take you until you explore. What people or causes in this world tug at your heart strings so much that you would love to find a way to help? Know that any act of kindness makes a difference, beyond what you could even imagine.

EDUCATION GIVES HOPE IN HAITI

Shad St Louis

My Smile and Your Smile

The smile on my face helps me forget my pain, the pain I've buried to survive.
The smile on my face is a raised fist—against pain and poverty.
My smile is a battle cry against hopelessness.
My smile says I will never stop trying.

But your smile . . . your smile is the dearest vision. It tells me of new hope.
My life has meaning because of the smile on your face.
Your smile says I have made a difference. Is there any greater joy?
Your smile is a reflection of mine and mine is a reflection of yours.
Let us rejoice.

I walked to school past dead people who were shot or ringed.[1] By whom? Why? File those questions away, I told myself. Education will free me, my mother had said over and over. Just keep walking and go to school. My mom slept with a machete to protect us—especially my sister—since girls were raped in the middle of the night. Many want to escape this land of so much pain and suffering, poverty and hopelessness.

I did escape, then felt compelled to return. Why? How do I sort through all of this pain? This pain that I've buried to survive. Where am I from? Haiti. It may not sound like it yet, but mine is a story of hope.

---

1   burned to death after a gasoline-filled tire around the neck is set aflame.

Please bear with me for a bit while I share my struggles, so that you will understand where I have come from. Then you will more fully appreciate the joy and pride of my accomplishments.

My name is Schadrac St Louis. People call me "Shad" or "Shasha." My father moved to the United States when I was an infant so that we could have a better life. He washed dishes, working wherever he could, and sending as much money as possible back to my mother, my sister, and me so that we would have a chance for a better life. There was not a lot of money to send, so my mother raised pigs to sell so that we could go to school. She instilled in my sister and me that education was the key to our freedom.

When I was twelve, I met my father for the first time that I could remember. He had returned to Haiti to file the paperwork to bring us, his family of four—soon to be five, then four—to the United States for a better life, a life of hope through education. I spent seven months with my father, getting to know the hardworking, honest man who sacrificed so much to make our life better, only to watch him die next to me during a car accident. I almost died myself, but no, I had to live to help my mom, who couldn't speak English, with a newborn infant to care for—my youngest brother, Samy.

I never knew what it was like to have a father, and to spend time with him. I felt like I grew up by myself. My mom, a single parent who lived from paycheck to paycheck, struggled in a country where she barely spoke the language. There were many choices and mistakes that were made and I would wonder: What would my father do? What would he say? I yearned for my father to offer me advice, but there was no father figure with a shoulder to cry on. I always had to be strong, to wear a mask of happiness.

When I help people with problems that are bigger than mine, my mountains of problems don't seem so high. I forget my own problems or set them aside. I feel better when I help people. I put so much energy and love into helping people because it helps me. My mother and aunt told me that, even as a young boy, I talked about helping children and poor people go to school.

Life in the States was not easy at first. I was learning the language, being teased in school, helping my mom fill out job applications, and translating for her when there were problems with money, all at the young age of fourteen. I survived by focusing on my education and helping my family survive the best that I could. I learned the language quickly and eventually made friends with a few white and Hispanic kids—not the African American kids, who looked like me. They teased me. (To this day, I am grateful to the teachers and counselors who encouraged me in school, especially Mrs. Filmore and Mrs. Pedri.)

I worked hard studying and, as soon as I was old enough, worked one, two, even three jobs to help my mom. I loved working hard and helping. I wanted to join the track team, but had to watch my younger brother while my mom worked. Finally, in my senior year of high school, my mom let me join the track team. I was a good runner and triple jumper—good enough that I earned a partial athletic scholarship to Alfred State College to study architectural design. I later transferred to Mercy College, where I earned a partial scholarship and studied English literature. After graduating with my bachelor's degree, I studied counseling. If education was my key to freedom, I knew that helping people was my medicine.

I earned my bachelor's, and started my master's degree, then worked at the attorney general's office as an intern. After that, I was hired as a counselor at Middletown High School. I became my own role model with the help of mentors. I realized that if my dad were alive, maybe it would have been different. Everything happens for a reason. I shape that reason to be what I want to be in life. I learned a lot working at the New York State Attorney General's office, working with John Katzenstein and Conrad Rutkowski. Conrad introduced me to Broadway, taking me to plays and musicals. I would drive him to the airport when he would go on vacation. He would pass things down to me, invite me for Thanksgiving, and talk to me and give me advice. I am so grateful for Conrad's mentoring.

After the earthquake in Haiti on January 12, 2010, I gathered a group of volunteers to assess the situation. We took the four-hour flight down, camped in a Catholic church courtyard, visited the tent camps, and handed out donations of basic necessities that we had brought with us on the plane. The country was chaotic. When we were walking out of the airport to catch a ride, people were begging. I made the mistake of giving a child a dollar, creating a mob scene of people trying to get more money from me. We wanted to help, but I certainly didn't want anyone to be hurt in the process, so had to learn safe ways to give.

When we brought donations to the tent village, we gave out numbers and people waited in line to receive a bag of clothes, water, and toiletries. When people are desperate from hunger and fear, they need help to act in a civilized manner so that everyone remains safe. Since I knew the language and people in Haiti, I was able to make connections so that our group of volunteers were transported safely and fed, and our tents were in a safe area. I was able to pay the local police to make sure that we were protected, because that was the situation at the time and I would not take any chances of my friends being hurt.

We took lots of pictures and videos from that trip to share with people when we returned. While we did see a lot of suffering in Haiti, what I did not see was the senseless violence that I had grown up with. This gave me hope that we could make a difference for the children and people in Haiti through education. The volunteers who joined me fell in love with the beautiful people in Haiti and were eager to continue helping.

Our first trip was made for the purpose of assessing the situation and offering donations during a time of crisis. When we returned, we shared our story with many people and gained mostly wonderful supporters who have been through some, or part, of this amazing journey. I say "mostly wonderful" because what I've learned through this process is that people offer to help for a variety of reasons. Many people give freely, straight from their heart; other people want to receive attention and recognition for giving, and that is their main motivation. The people who were looking for recognition served a purpose by sharing our project through the media and other channels, which brought us funds and support. However, problems arose when fundraisers gained more attention than money, due to poor management. Some big supporters from the beginning got worn out and, instead of bowing out gracefully, caused a great deal of drama. (I'll share more details later in my story.)

Now, about the person who played a big role in this cause and my life. Have you read Carina's story yet? Then you know some of what happened. We knocked down and rebuilt a school for the children three times, each time learning more.

Our vision was to have a school that could help students in Haiti and in the United States, to have a strong cultural exchange, and to make sure that the students were learning.

The first school was on my relatives' property, which they legally signed over to us freely—we thought. The night before the school opening in October 2010, my relative sat down with us to ask for $1,000 a month rent for the property. How embarrassing and disheartening. We had barely scraped together enough money to ship the donated buildings to Haiti, along with paying all the bribes to get the buildings through customs. We had no extra money.

There is a perception, in Haiti, that money grows on trees in the United States. My relatives were convinced that all the volunteers who visited were giving me a lot of money. The truth was that I was funding a lot of their trip by paying people to cook for us, to bribe the police, and much more. While I was earning $50,000 a year as a counselor, my money went to food, rent, flights to Haiti, and other expenses. I was broke.

Despite this bump in the road—which felt more like a huge mountain at the time—the school opened the next day. The children had beautiful uniforms, backpacks, and classrooms. The former Haitian Ambassador attended our opening ceremonies, played his harmonica, and sang with the children, as well as speaking to everyone. He asked the children to:

- replace "Mwen pa konnen" ("I don't know") with "Mwen konnen." ("I know"), and
- replace "Mwen pa ka" ("I can't") with "Mwen pral eseye" ("I will try").

We had school on my relatives' property, but soon had to move the buildings to my mother's house in the middle of the night to get away from our relatives' demands for money. Working as a counselor in the States while running a school in Haiti was extremely stressful, but I felt alive because my dream of helping children through education was coming true. Even before the earthquake, I saw people who were desperate, longing for something different, but not knowing what path to take to find that "something different." That fueled me into action to get support. People were so generous and that is how it all started. That is how I decided to move to Haiti.

I was inspired to make a difference for those people who were suffering from the same issues that I have faced—and mostly overcome—in my life. I say "mostly" because the truth is that I volunteered myself back into poverty when I moved to my mom's house in Haiti so that I could oversee and continue to build the school and community. I felt it was the next thing that I had to do, to see if I could make a difference. I wondered if we could create something out of nothing with a vision. Could we put our differences aside, regardless of our political views, whether black or white, and make this a reality? Honestly we did.

We put someone's interests above our own and were able to make our vision a reality, through many twists, turns, and bumps in the road. As you know, Carina moved down at that same time to volunteer with me. I feared for her safety, addressing rumors immediately that men wanted to harm her. I wouldn't allow her to go out of our gated compound by herself (although she did not always listen, which worried and frustrated me). The last thing that I wanted was for this generous, adventurous young lady to get hurt.

So much at that time was up in the air and chaotic. Donations were just barely covering our costs. We were living in tents on the roof of my mom's house and the former school buildings while we set up the school in the house downstairs. People would expect things from me that I couldn't give and they would not believe me. People came to me for help with legitimate concerns about basic necessities like health issues, or not having food or decent shelter. I had to prioritize who I could and couldn't help, which at times was heartbreaking. I learned that some of the loudest people were not in need, so I watched for the people quietly suffering and did my best to help them.

In December of 2011, a woman came to us with an oozing tumor the size of a soccer ball on her leg. I wasn't a doctor, nor did I have the funds to pay for a doctor. I did have a car, though, so we drove her from clinic to clinic, receiving rejection after rejection. Carina learned that the tumor needed to be cleaned every day to keep an infection at bay, so she helped the woman's daughter to clean the wound daily until she was able to have surgery. The woman and her daughter's strength, hope, and positive attitude were amazing. People in the States helped, too, finding a surgeon in the States who was coming down to Haiti and agreed to amputate her leg. To this day, I would like to say thank you to each person who saved a beautiful woman and mother's life that Haitian doctors would not help. It was a very challenging time, but the ending was really positive.

Through the help of many people, we were able to raise enough funds to purchase two acres of property in Merger, a town just a mile from my house. Land was cleared, architects drew plans for a beautiful school, and $20,000 was raised to put in a solid foundation created by hired Haitian people and volunteers. We were bringing much-needed jobs to hard-working Haitian people. Things were looking up. Then we hit the lowest point of this journey when our initial team of supporters started questioning everything that we were doing and, eventually, completely pulled out their support, leaving us with an unfinished foundation, taking away the not for profit status which helped us to receive large donations. We had no money to pay the teachers or feed the children— or our Haitian team, Carina, or myself.

Before that, we could at least count on having a bowl of beans and rice each day, but we couldn't even count on this basic necessity. I remember working all day in the hot sun building the school with our team on the new property and returning to have no food for dinner. Knowing that we had no money in our account, we could have just left. I would have gone if Carina had said "Let's go," but she did not. Carina wanted to stay to see if we could keep the school going. I had to scrap metal in exchange for money to feed the kids. I put my head down to beg for money from our new group of supporters. To add insult to injury, even though I had no money, some people in the Haitian community were spreading rumors that I had money, which I wasn't sharing, claiming that I could do more. They thought I was lying. Everything was crashing.

There was a division between myself and my two right-hand men, Dieumaitre and Adam. I knew that we needed to sit down and talk, so I scheduled a meeting. They talked about money that I had never seen. I had been hiding the truth of what was going on with our finances from them because I didn't want Adam and Dieumaitre to feel discouraged that there was no money. I had been keeping a smile on my face as if everything was okay so that they wouldn't worry. I couldn't pretend any longer with all of the lies breaking my team apart. Once I shared the bank balances and emails with them, they once again trusted me—and our bond as friends and leaders was strengthened. Over time, they realized that I was not making sacrifices for myself, I was making them for us, for our community. I want people to see that I led by example.

Because the school was at my house, with volunteers coming and going—and no money—chaos ensued. One volunteer sent out an email to many people involved, pointing out all the things that were wrong with the school and my house. I was afraid that my dear friends, Mike and Allison Wilbur, and the Otisville church were ready to walk away from the project because of this email. I wanted to hide under a blanket, but instead I called Mike and explained my view. We talked about it. I started making excuses about the state of my house, saying that we were focusing on the school. Mike encouraged me to find truth in what the letter said and address those issues. I vowed to make changes in how my house was kept. I realized that people cared about both the school and our house, which was beautiful. We were working so hard to help people, we forgot to take care of ourselves. Little by little, we made changes. Carina put in gardens. She continued to be patient with everyone, which helped me to be less cynical. And I am happy to say that Mike and Allison visited recently and said that my house had gone from a negative-two-star to a four-star establishment.

We built a new group of supporters and HEART, the Haiti Education and Resource Team, was born. This transition brought us much-needed structure and gave transparency to how our funds were being used. We can now show that money was only allocated for projects to help the children's education, not plane tickets or hotel rooms for board members or fundraisers that raised no funds. Now, to be part of bringing people on the board who are putting the kids' interests first, like Carina and I have always done, is remarkable. It is beyond words that we could make that happen. Carina and I were able to pull people together and make something out of nothing. Despite the fact that we lost our not-for-profit status, so many people stayed with us and new, highly valuable supporters joined as well.

Dick Martin, a retired professor from the College of Architecture at Georgia Tech, visited us in April 2011 and was so impressed with how well we were doing at operating an elementary school out of an unfinished house that he made our school his project. Dick was able to purchase and convert four forty-foot shipping containers into classrooms, a cafeteria, and a kitchen. The containers were placed on simple concrete foundations, and his design for the roof allows for air flow across the top of the containers, making the interior cooler in spite of the intense Haitian sun. Voilà. We had a real school.

The HEART school was constructed on the new two-acre property, which allowed us to open the school on time in October 2012. Before and after Dick's passing, his wife, Barbara Rose, a member of the Midtown Atlanta Rotary Club, has been a fantastic support to us. She has raised funds to cover the complete cost of the school building from Rotary clubs in New York, Georgia, and Bulgaria, in addition to many contributions from individuals. Ms. Rose's company, New Generation Partnerships, Inc. trains not-for-profit boards around the world to work effectively as a team and raise funds for their organizations, and her guidance has helped us to build a board that is organized and empowered.

After more than two years of volunteering in Haiti, the HEART board had enough financial stability to offer a salary to Carina and myself. Up to this point, only the teachers and Haitian staff had been paid. While $175 a month is not a lot of money for me to be paid, it was much better than nothing. Carina's salary was $125 a month. We used our salaries to fix up the house and treat ourselves to a dinner out every now and then.

A lot of people in Haiti are doing little or nothing to improve their situations. I know this comes from an attitude of hopelessness. I wanted to be a role model for people to learn that they can do something and make a difference. Adam and Dieumaitre have seen how hard I worked not only during the week, but also on weekends. They see how all of this hard work paid off in creating the school. They also work hard during the week, plus get an education on the weekends to better themselves. They have the same problems as I, since Dieumaitre is an orphan and Adam has to take care of his family. But it is the choices that people make in their lives that shape their futures. I am so proud of all that Adam and Dieumaitre have accomplished. They started a vocational school in the afternoons, teaching adults construction, architecture, plumbing, electricity, and English. This school is funded from the students' tuition. In the summer of 2013, Carina and I were hired by them and paid to teach English at their school. To see people that I have mentored create a successful program, then turn around and hire me, is inspiring.

We are empowering a handful of people and are working to empower more. I've learned from experience how important it is to listen to people. In the beginning, I would do most of the talking at meetings. Then I would have our head teacher, Patricia, run half of the meeting. Over time, I pulled out slowly, empowering Patricia in her role as head teacher.

I've learned from Maria Blon, who has been a steady supporter through this entire journey of building the school and training the teachers, how to reframe questions when the teachers ask what they should do. I will turn their questions around and ask them how they think the problem could be solved. I keep the teachers informed about what happens behind the scenes (for example, telling them that board members who fund our school are coming down to visit). The more people know, the more that they are empowered. We listen to each other and come up with solutions together. In one situation, one of the teacher's aides was feeling like the teachers were making fun of her when she cleaned up the children if they had an accident. We had a meeting with the teachers and talked about what an important role she plays at the school, helping everybody respect and value each other. At another time, I made laminated signs with all of the teachers' names and posted them on each of the classrooms. Our school assistant was in tears, because her name was not displayed anywhere at the school. At first I thought, "My name isn't up anywhere, but that doesn't bother me." But I realized that it is important to value people in a way that they appreciate. That was a simple problem to solve. I realized, "Why not have everyone's names up on the wall?" Since I am approachable, people feel safe telling me what is and is not working. One parent couldn't afford to buy her child's books. I asked her to spend a week working at the school in exchange for the books. Jesula, the school custodian, was excited to have an assistant. They worked together, made a great team, and divided the work.

We have learned that the training and regular evaluation of teachers builds effective teachers and cultivates students who are able to learn and solve problems using critical thinking. This Chinese proverb guides me and Carina in our work:

"If you are planning for a year, sow rice; if you are planning for a decade, plant trees; if you are planning for a lifetime, educate people."

We have coordinated several professional development trainings for the teachers thanks to: Joanne Lee, Judy Rector, Maria Blon, Allison Wilbur, and Art Reach. The French movies, *Today is the day* and *The Chorus* have been wonderful education tools that have inspired the teachers.

When I see the students coming to school, happy to be there, I feel wonderful. Children like Dayanka and Richardson, who were initially so shy, are now comfortable in their classroom. When a white person used to visit the school, the kids would fight, putting their hands out, asking to be given something. Now they sit down and are polite. They don't beg anymore. They know that every day, they get a meal. They can relax and there is no need to fight for food. The children used to push and fight, fearful that the food might run out. Now they feel secure, because they know each person will be fed each day. It is wonderful to see the children coming to the school happy. Many children have been treated badly but, at the school, they have a safe place.

Sometimes, though, I feel powerless. We helped one family a tremendous amount, but the father of the family had mental health issues. One day, he started cursing out other parents while he was waiting to pick up his daughter. He was being so rude that I was called to the school's gate. He cursed me out in front of the parents, which was embarrassing.

He said that white people gave $5,000 when his son died and that I had kept half of the money—which of course was not true. This family had received medical care and tremendous support and a new house when his son died, yet he doesn't have the slightest bit of appreciation for what was done for him, and instead he throws anger and a sense of entitlement at me. His family is ashamed of his behavior, but powerless to control his tyrannical ways. In the time since he caused the uproar at our gates, he has un-enrolled his daughter from the school, which is heartbreaking. She was really happy at school, and is such a joyful child who had learned so much and created wonderful friendships at the school. Thankfully, that man is a rare exception. Mostly I am in awe of the strength that Haitian people show despite great hardship.

At the school, we have a great team that works well together. Rosita, for instance, has such a beautiful smile, gently takes care of her own—and other people's—children, is only just making it, yet always finds ways to help people. She is full of life and very appreciative. Families that are struggling financially somehow find a way to earn enough money to purchase books for their students. When I walk through Merger, people come to me sharing how appreciative they are that we brought the school to their community. They welcome visitors into their town because we have taken the time to build relationships with these people and show that we care. Carina was a big part of building these relationships when she interviewed families to see if their children would be a good fit for the school.

Carina left Haiti in 2014 to attend college in the States. The teachers miss Carina and her smile. I am happy to hear that. I ask if they are living by her example. Rosita often asks how Carina is, and I help her Skype with Carina. The kids constantly ask about Carina, as well. She means a lot to them. One of the students, Richardson, was telling everyone that Carina was sick. I had to dispel his rumors and tell the children the truth that—although Carina had been sick—she is now going to school in the States. Of course, they want to know when she is coming back. They feel privileged to hear stories of Carina.

Our pre-K students and kindergarteners are our best students because, to educate future leaders, we have to get them young in order to shape their minds. We encourage the habits of working hard and sharing.

I see many young people making bad choices and know I am lucky that I had my mother's guidance. When I was young, I could have been involved with a bad crowd, but I made a choice to work hard and find refuge in education to make something of myself. Helping young people to see how they can fill the void to make even a little bit of change in their lives is empowering to them—and to me. The school is our number one priority. I've had more arguments with Carina about the school than about our personal life. We are passionate about helping, making a difference, and making sure that the children are our number one priority.

I feel happy that I can relate to people who are having trouble by disclosing what I have gone through. Helping people to make changes and show them how much they have which they take for granted is empowering. I like to share my life experiences with people to help them see new options for their lives—to give people hope. Without hope, there can be no progress, because nobody will try. When things are really bad, people can't move forward until they can see the *possibility of improvement*, and that's what hope really is. The wondrous thing that I've found is that hope is something you can actually give to someone else. When life is full of horror and suffering, every single person who is willing to keep trying can inspire hope in the people around them. My mother was right about education—in many ways, it will free you. And nothing can be accomplished without hard work. But hope is the key to everything.

Shad's Lesson: Persevering to Give Hope

Shad's wise realization that hope through education is the key to empowering people in Haiti, and his perseverance through obstacle after obstacle, inspires me to be a better person. Having seen and played a supporting role during some of what he has gone through, I am grateful that Shad has included me and especially Carina in helping his homeland.

Every time I visit Shad and the school, great improvements have been made to the buildings and grounds. The teachers are kind to their students, encouraging them to learn critical thinking skills. Shad empowers people through his example of listening, treating people with respect, forgiving those who have caused him pain, working hard, and trying new ideas. Shad has persevered through many challenges, modeling how education offers hope!

Reflection

How many opportunities can you find in a day to do something kind for a person that you meet? Notice how you feel when helping someone and the effect your kindness has on them.

Imagine how Shad would have felt if he had given up when the money ran out before the school was built. Contrast this with how much pride he must feel after persevering and successfully building the school. In what areas of your life do you feel like giving up but could instead practice perseverance to make your dream become reality?

Transforming Past Trauma through Self-Inquiry Healing

Melanie Wood

Friend: Have you?
Me: Have I what? Found my reason? (for living)
Friend: Yes.
Me: Yes. I found my "why" in the magic of what I do . . . the unexplainable that happens just because I show up.

I love that I am proud of myself for this—holding space—it is magical. It doesn't "look" like I am doing anything—in groups, individually, for myself, but on a whole—it is powerful . . . it is my form of giving grace to the world . . . and it is necessary.

Conviction.

Looking at rolling mountains, green and fresh, with sweet air and a breathtaking blue sky is normally a source of exhilarating happiness for me, sometimes even a much-needed escape from the stress and reality of responsibility in life. On one particular day, however, a deep sense of fear, loneliness, sadness and longing enveloped my senses. I looked at my partner, wondering if I should break the mood. He was holding my hand and had a peaceful smile tugging at his lips. Without warning, tears started rolling down my cheeks. My partner heard my breath catch in my throat and looked at me with alarm. His eyes asked me what was wrong. I, as usual, struggled to put words to the raw emotion I was feeling. It took me a moment to piece together phrases that had a chance of making sense.

There is a place very deep inside of me, a place that I am not conscious of every day, where my deep, childhood roots live. On this day, my roots decided to show themselves, triggered by the view. It was the mountains. They brought to mind another set of mountains from my childhood, long ago. And, without warning, I was back there, in a dark, lonely place. An intense longing for emotional warmth and physical comfort engulfed me as I was thrown back into my traumatic childhood. I was an abused child, with no sense of security, no trust, and a strong desire to escape.

What was happening that day with my partner is psychologically defined as an emotional trigger. I can experience intense emotional and physical responses to these triggers, especially if I feel like I am in a place of safety. It is a sort of paradox that I am best able to remember and experience some past trauma when I am feeling most safe and secure. In this case, my partner's warmth and acceptance of me, along with his own trusting personality, enabled me to feel safe enough to bring back a whirlwind of very strong feelings.

I have experienced recurring triggers over much of my life—they are the result of an unfortunate history. I now have the awareness, knowledge, and experience to be able to explain what happened to trigger my emotions, which is deeply healing for me. This was not always the case. I went from being an abused child to being a teenage runaway, followed by engaging in a series of abusive relationships. As an adult, I continued to make choices that kept me a victim. This is clear to me now. In *dis*-comfort, I found a perverse comfort, for the abusive pattern was most familiar to me, predictable, and constant.

Eventually, I started desiring a different way of living. More and more shifts in my awareness occurred until I found myself in active pursuit of physical, emotional and spiritual cleansing and healing. I participated in healing modalities and spiritual education for many years. Life got better. Bad habits and patterns began to disappear as I made conscious and intentional decisions.

But even after making changes in my living environment and career, the way I cared for my body, and how I used techniques to cope with emotional and mental stress—and actively seeking a spiritual lifestyle—

triggers would creep in (and still do). After months or years of thinking that something I had repressed, avoided, or ignored had been released, an emotional or physical trigger might still emerge, just as strong as in the past. Living with these triggers brought up so many questions:

- How deep is the trauma still living within me?
- Does it ever go away?
- How much work is needed to break the barriers that are blocking me from completely healing from the trauma?
- Is this possible to do while still maintaining a regular lifestyle with family, work and fun?
- What kind of impact do the effects of trauma have on realizing and actualizing my authentic potential?
- And, lastly, am I even supposed to know the answers to these questions?

Self Inquiry

I'd learned that sometimes, when you can form really good questions, they can function as bridges to the answers themselves. And I knew that, with vital questions like the ones listed above it was time I took a long, honest look at myself. I finally admitted that being a teenage runaway and experiencing all the trauma from that time of my life was continuing to affect me, primarily in the feeling of wanting to run. Sometimes quite literally, my body urgently wanted to run down the road, or run out the door. At other times, I just wanted to escape from whatever stress was most recently occurring.

Though I have never been diagnosed with Post Traumatic Stress Disorder, my symptoms are so similar to PTSD that I wondered about whether that was what I was experiencing. Could my self-inquiry give me insights into the effects of traumatic stress and put me on the path to healing?

The desire to perform intensive self-inquiry had been brewing for some time and the running provided a starting place for me. As an adult, my body still frequently had an insatiable urge to run, although I absolutely hated the actual practice of running. I could clearly see that

I was a runner in other areas of my life, too—I ran from relationships that got too close, I ran from other opportunities to be vulnerable, I ran from healthy career and academic choices. Was I running *toward* something? It felt like I was constantly looking for something "better," running toward what would satisfy me, but I never found it. I understood that running away in my early years was a defense and survival mechanism (because I had to leave an abusive household). But why, as an adult, did I still have the urge to run?

Somatic bodywork sessions, primarily Mindful Movement and Meditation with reflection and self-inquiry (as found in Phoenix Rising Yoga Therapy), helped me to realize the very distinct connection between my emotional state and my life circumstances. It was not until recently (in the last few years prior to this writing) that I realized my behavior patterns, my resurfacing emotional patterns, my unconscious cellular reactions, and other blocks to potential could indeed be released with somatic work. As I learned more and read important works like *In An Unspoken Voice: How the Body Releases Trauma and Restores Goodness* by Peter Levine, I became hopeful that by listening to my body and making conscious decisions based on the information stored within it, my trauma-related effects could be healed.

After much thought and study, I decided to explore my "running urge" in a most extreme way. In January of 2012, I committed to training to run a marathon. I wanted my body to give me answers, even in the hurt muscles, toxic fatigue, exhaustion, and nausea that ensued.

I was not surprised at the result of my marathon training. My body did speak. Physical pain and imbalances that had nothing to do with the miles, along with flashbacks, nightmares, and visions in meditations were just some of my companions on the road toward 26.2 miles. I acknowledged and listened to what was happening. As I grew stronger in my body, I could feel the result of trauma being released from my cells. I could feel myself becoming free.

My life began to change, too. Fear of commitment began to ease. It was released and replaced with confidence, love, a desire to be vulnerable and settled, and most importantly, a glimpse of who my Authentic Self is. I was finally honest with everyone around me. I committed to one romantic partner, worked on resigning from jobs that no longer served me, started graduate school, became a more patient parent, and decided I was just fine living in a small town full of unknown potential. I focused on becoming my best Self—not simply running from myself. I learned so much from training for this marathon and working on my self inquiry that I will be forever grateful for this experience.

I trained hard until race day. Unfortunately, before the end of the marathon (after 18.5 miles) I injured myself and could not finish the race. I had to admit that I could no longer run and needed to allow myself to be taken care of by my partner, who happens to be a physical therapist. (Oh, the irony.) I stopped to heal, hibernate, and reflect. I stopped training; I stopped looking for what else could be released. I focused on recovering, both from the injury and from the insight into the lasting traumatic effects of my past. This was the perfect outcome. I am no longer a runner—in every sense of the word. Mission accomplished.

This experience fueled my desire to find out what else was stored in my body and was blocking potential and optimum well-being. Thus, I decided to do heuristic research on myself for my Capstone project in graduate school. Reading more from author Peter Levine, I learned that my experience was, indeed, a somatic release of trauma. I learned that the insatiable desire to physically run was my body enticing me to pay attention to, and self-regulate, my stored emotions and behaviors. Committing to paying attention to the sensations in my body and acting on these sensations eventually did provide me with relief and balance, both in my life and in my body. It was refreshing to read about the innate human capacity for recovery. I am intrigued by the delicate simplicity and ease that simply paying attention can offer.

One of the most amazing things that I discovered when training to run long distances was my body's capacity to work in such extreme conditions. Reflecting on this was a catalyst for thoughts and memories of physical and emotional pain caused by the abuse when I was younger. Discovering the strength that I had developed over the years by surviving difficult situations was an incredible breakthrough moment. I had lived with self-doubt and disappointment and had never seen the strength inside me. Now I know it was always there, growing in the form of resilience. I have developed a deep sense of gratitude and respect for my own strength.

Reading about how the body stores information in such a grand physiological way also produced some fear within me. I understood that I could come across memories that have been repressed and forgotten. Already aware of some traumatic memories, it was a scary notion to imagine what else could be unearthed. Despite the fear, however, I knew the process of discovery was necessary.

Although there continues to be a chance of tiny to intense trauma happening daily, I want to find a way to be free from the past. I know from experience that listening to somatic sensations is the key way for this to happen. My Capstone project is finished, but I continue with my passion for self-inquiry—not only to continue to heal myself, but to help others heal and discover their own hidden strengths. Today, I share my experiences of self-healing with you. If this writing resonated with you, thank you for allowing me to be your model.

Love,

Melanie Autumn Wood

Melanie's Lesson: Authenticity

One of my hardest challenges in life is taking deep and honest looks right at myself. What I love so much about Melanie is her willingness to do this repeatedly, and to be vulnerable, sharing her emotions and thoughts around sensitive issues in her life. Melanie does this in person, with her students and clients, and even on Facebook. I can always count on Melanie to be authentic. I am impressed with her drive to keep learning and growing amidst life challenges. She is smart, brave, honest, and open about her growth. Her courage to heal and share her healing in order to help people is inspiring.

This quote by Oriah Mountain Weaver reminds me of the courage Melanie shows as she shares her deepest hurts along with her greatest triumphs:

It doesn't interest me what you do for a living. I want to know what you ache for, and if you dare to dream of meeting your heart's longing.

It doesn't interest me how old you are. I want to know if you will risk looking like a fool for love, for your dream, for the adventure of being alive.

Reflection

Do you, like Melanie, experience emotions which seem to be disconnected from what is happening in the present moment? Does it feel like these may be old emotions or stories resurfacing from the past?

Consider noticing what is happening with your emotions, along with the sensations in your body, and recording what you observe. Are there areas of your life that are calling for a closer look, even some self-inquiry? Would you like support through this process from a friend or trusted professional? Healing occurs best in a safe environment where you can be your authentic self.

Blessing the Bumpy Ride and Going with the Flow

Sheila Pearl

My passions began as little sparks, little hints of who I was born to be, little peeks of the pieces of the divine essence planted inside of my DNA. When I was seven, I remember Mama asking me, "So, honey, what do you want to be when you grow up?" I looked up at my mama's sweet face feeling so loved, as she smiled at me. "I want to be just like YOU; I want to be a singer and a mom—just like YOU."

Already, as a seven-year-old child, I knew who I was and what I wanted to become. Yes, my mother was my role model; but I somehow recognized myself in her. I sensed that I was destined to be a nurturer (mother) and to use my voice (as a singer). From that early age, my passions motivated me to take action on my dreams, and what I would learn much later in life was that our passions often lead us to outcomes we never would have imagined! It has been the driving force of my passions which has given me the strength to overcome many adversities and challenges, and to eventually learn to bless the bumpy road called life. I would learn that it was that "bumpy road" which was the greatest blessing of all, that every challenge was happening *for* me . . . not *to* me.

I was born into a musical family; Mama and Daddy were professional singers and musicians. Every day was filled with music and singing. At the age of five, I appeared on a radio show with my parents and we won first prize in a talent competition. My mama kept telling me that we won because I was so adorable. She always found ways to let me know I was special. When I was six, I began piano lessons, and was singing all the time. I loved learning to play new songs; one of my favorites was "Somewhere Over the Rainbow" from *The Wizard of Oz*.

At my first recital, when I was nine, I sang that song. All of a sudden, in the middle of singing my favorite song, my mind went blank—I forgot the words! I was trembling and imagined that everyone would laugh at me, but I looked out at the audience and Mama was sitting in the front row, smiling at me. Like a lightning flash, I remembered what she had said to me many times: "Whenever you're singing a song and you forget the words, just make them up. Don't ever stop . . . just keep singing!" So I rolled with it—I made it all up and didn't stop singing. When I finished the song, taking my bow, I received my very first standing ovation. My two proud parents, with tears running down their cheeks as they were smiling at me, were vigorously clapping their hands!

Forgetting the words and singing the rest of "Somewhere Over the Rainbow" was the beginning of my journey in leaning into a situation and not running away, not quitting, not giving up. Mama had taught me the wisdom of "going with the flow" and jumping into the middle of the river, letting go of the shore. I didn't know it then, but my mama was preparing me for facing life's challenges. She was my greatest teacher and guide in ways I would appreciate decades later. While I began to practice "going with the flow" as a young child, I had not yet learned about the wisdom of the Hopi Elders, who urge us all to "let go of the shore." In one of the messages from the Hopi Elders, they remind us that "there is a river flowing now very fast" and that we must "push off into the middle of the river . . ." and "let go of the shore."

During several major, challenging events in my life, I would be faced with a question: Is there really going to be a "pot of gold" at the end of the rainbow? Is there any blessing or lesson in this painful situation? In the midst of challenges, my faith in what was at the end of that rainbow and my ability to "let go of the shore" would be tested, decade after decade, and triumph after defeat after triumph.

The first test was my recital when I was nine. One year after that recital, something happened that shook my world. I felt like life was happening *to* me. I wasn't ready to fully understand that life is always happening *for* me. What happened? My parents divorced. When my mama first uttered the word "divorce," I felt my world collapse. Yet, in that moment, I made an important decision: I decided that when I got married someday, I would never *ever* get a divorce. Looking back on that awful event in my life, I now realize that a seed was planted at that moment for me to find a way to help people build and maintain loving relationships so that they could prevent divorce. *Know the river has its destination . . .*

Push off into the middle of the river . . . After my parents divorced and my little brother and I were living with Mama in a separate house away from my father, I continued to sing. My father was a voice teacher and I wanted his approval. I practiced my piano and my vocal exercises diligently, sacrificing spending time with my friends after school so I could practice as much as possible. *Somewhere over the rainbow bluebirds fly . . . why, oh why, can't I?* In high school, I was in all the school musicals and concerts, getting solos in everything. My chorus teacher recommended me for a television program, *Spotlight on Youth*, and I appeared with some celebrities on the show, representing my high school. Everyone was so proud.

My vision was clear. I was focusing on becoming an opera singer. After graduating high school, my mother and stepfather moved with my brother and me up to the San Francisco Bay Area. While I was in college, as a music major, I heard from my music professor about the San Francisco Opera Talent Bank. I auditioned for the Talent Bank and was accepted. *Somewhere over the rainbow . . .* Those of us who were in that elite group were like a junior company for the San Francisco Opera—we were sent out to the local communities to perform concert-style operatic solos and duets and ensemble segments. We performed for schools, in libraries, and on radio programs. It was the beginning of my career. I was on my way! . . . *why, oh why, can't I?*

Then something happened . . . . I was in my junior year of college and—up to that point in my life—had remained celibate; I didn't want to take a chance of getting pregnant like many of my high school friends. Oh, no! I would take precautions against that happening by saying "No!" to any seductive attempt by the young men in my life. I never dreamed that I would have to go to my mother to tell her the unthinkable . . . but I did. I had to tell my mama something I couldn't believe: I was pregnant. I had had sex with Sheldon once and quickly regretted it, sure that since it was my first time, I wouldn't get pregnant. There was a conspiracy, it seems, because the chances of my getting pregnant were millions to one. I was the "one." It was not good timing for someone who had her sights fixed on an operatic career and wasn't even graduated from college yet! . . . *let go of the shore* . . .

Was I surprised when Mama's response to my devastating news was: "Honey . . . we'll handle this together." Sheldon wanted to marry me, but I wasn't sure if I wanted to marry him. Mama and my stepfather both supported whatever decision I chose to make. I decided not to marry Sheldon. Mama, my stepfather, and my brother stood by me. When I brought my baby daughter home from the hospital, my family had moved into a larger house so that I would have my own apartment on the third floor. I named my daughter Daedra; she awakened every morning cooing and singing. She was a precious gift to us all; Mama and the rest of my family fell in love with my sweet child. She became the centerpiece of our lives. I put both my college career and my singing career on hold. I was totally dedicated to being "mama" and every day was a delight.

One brisk March morning, when Daedra was eight months old, soon after I had dropped her at the babysitter's and arrived at work, I got a call: "Come get Daedra now; she's having trouble breathing!" I felt my pulse racing as I left work to pick her up. Before leaving my office, I called our family doctor and he told me to come straight to the hospital where he was. As I was driving my baby to Dr. Pat's office at the hospital, she was gasping for air, sweating, and looking over at me, repeating "Mama! . . . Mama!" My heart was pounding as I was driving. It seemed like forever before I got to the hospital. Dr. Pat was waiting for me at the ER entrance. "Give her to me, honey. I'll bring her home to you later. Go home and put your feet up." Three hours later, the doorbell rang. It was Dr. Pat. He was standing there with tears running down his cheeks. I knew. "We did everything we could . . . she's gone." Daedra had been born with a congenital heart defect; her heart was a fibrous tissue, not a muscle. She had been designed to live no more than a year. At that moment, I knew what hell was about. *Somewhere over the rainbow* . . . How does anyone survive the pain of the loss of a child? *Let go of the shore* . . .

At the age of twenty-three, I had learned a wealth of wisdom in a flash: 1) there are no guarantees; 2) everything is on loan; and, 3) the only certainty in life is uncertainty.

We all mourned the loss of Daedra.

Three months after Daedra's passing, Mama came to me with an envelope of cash: "I want you to go to New York. I want you to follow your dream. Sing your heart out!" One of my best friends from college was in New York and gave me a place to stay. I got a job at the World's Fair and began to study voice, learning operatic repertoire, and being coached to learn Italian, French, and German diction for singing the major operatic roles. After a few months in New York, I received a call that my father was dying of cancer, and I returned to California. After my father's passing, I decided to stay in California and complete my final year of college. After graduation, I returned to New York to resume my pursuit of an operatic career. It was a bumpy road. Lots of rejections. Lots of disappointments. And lots of triumphs as well. *Somewhere over the rainbow . . .*

My longing for children was digging into my heart; I became obsessed with finding a husband. I wanted to have my babies—my heart was bleeding from the loss of my child and I couldn't stop thinking about having children. Somehow—I didn't know how—I would find a husband and have my big house with lots of children! *Jump into the river . . . let go of the shore . . .*

It was a cold November afternoon. I was working on a project for my job and was preparing for an audition the next day. My roommate called and interrupted my practicing, saying: "I want you to meet my new boyfriend who's here from Israel with some of the other journalists. Come meet us for drinks and dinner tonight at the Waldorf." I wore my black turtleneck sheath dress, high boots, and a purple "diva" coat lined with black lambswool. In those days I was a size ten, with long blond hair, and people often described me as "the blonde bombshell." I was trained to walk like a diva who is six feet tall (although I'm only 5'4") and, as I walked into the lobby of the Waldorf Astoria, I felt someone staring at me. Diane waved to me as I walked over to her table. The eyes I had felt staring at me were Aaron's. He was looking at me as if he had seen a ghost—I immediately didn't like him; I was spooked.

. . . And the dreams we dare to dream, . . . oh why, oh why, can't I? . . .
As crazy as it sounds, Aaron knew the moment he saw me that
he wanted to marry me. He told my roommate as I was walking toward
them that he was going to marry me someday. Diane laughed at him.
Aaron had the last laugh—I married him two years later.

. . . Jump into the river . . . let go of the shore . . . Shortly before Aaron
and I were to be married, his oldest son left for a date and never came
home. The car accident was a reminder that everything is on loan, and
the only certainty in life is uncertainty. The death of Aaron's eldest son
was a tragedy felt by all of us for many years. Aaron couldn't imagine
starting a new family; he was broken and would not allow me to talk
about getting pregnant. For him, it was unthinkable. For me, it was the
death of my dream to have my babies. *Somewhere over the rainbow . . .*
Aaron's two other children came to live with us; I became a stepmother
to two angry and troubled teenagers. Our domestic life was filled with
conflict. *Let go of the shore . . .* I wanted to leave, but I had promised myself I would never divorce.

. . . why, oh why, can't I? . . . I found a family therapist who helped us
all learn better ways of managing conflict; she also inspired me to return
to school. I put my operatic aspirations on hold while I worked to earn
my master's degree in clinical social work. If I wasn't going to have my
own babies, perhaps I could use my nurturing capacities to serve people
who needed what I could offer of myself. Often my sweet mother would
say to me: "The people who are the most unlovable need the most love . .
. Go love them!" Instead of bringing more babies into the world, I shifted
my focus from being a mother to my own children to being a stepmother
to my husband's children and nurturer to others I would serve as a social
worker and therapist.

Somewhere over the rainbow bluebirds fly . . . why, oh why, can't I?
I couldn't live without singing. I fell into a deep depression and I knew
that I had cut off a part of me that needed to live. Part of my passion
was nurturing. But it was also singing—using my voice. The last year of
graduate school, I lifted my spirits back up by planning my debut recital at Carnegie Recital Hall. I planned my program and began studying
with my teachers again. I felt myself coming back to life. I was living my

passion. I felt the juices of energy and excitement flowing throughout my body and spirit once again.

In June 1981, I graduated from Wurzweiler School of Social Work, earning my master's degree and I also received rave reviews from the *New York Times* for my recital debut at Carnegie. As soon as I was sending out my resume to seek a job using my M.S.W., my husband lost his job. We had two teenagers at home and I had student loans to pay. I couldn't afford to take an entry-level job as a social worker. It felt like life kept throwing me curve balls. It felt like life was happening *to* me . . . and I didn't like feeling like a victim. *Somewhere over the rainbow* . . . I refused to give up on my dream!

What happened to my dream of a big house with lots of children?

I was working at a job I didn't like but was making enough money to take care of my family. My husband got a part-time pulpit job serving a small congregation as its rabbi. Their former rabbi had also been their cantor; so when they hired Aaron, they also needed to hire a cantor. Aaron convinced them to take a chance on me as their cantorial soloist for Rosh Hashana and Yom Kippur. I was a quick study. Heck— I'd learned to sing in Italian, French, German, Swedish, and Russian. I certainly could learn to sing the Hebrew. Aaron and his former cantor trained me, in just eight weeks, to sing the music for the High Holidays. To my amazement, I loved it! I had never done that kind of thing before, so I had no idea how it would feel being a cantor. Working with my husband was also a dream come true. I had known hell. Now I knew heaven.

While barely tolerating my day job, I also kept working with my voice teacher and coaches, giving concerts and performing in regional opera performances. I knew if I just stayed in motion, keeping my eye on my passion, I would somehow find a way to live my dream. I just didn't know *how* . . .

"I've just heard about a cantorial job that would be perfect for you." It was Jacob, my friend and cantorial teacher. He put me in touch with a congregation in New Jersey that was looking for a good singer. Jacob told me I was up against graduates of the cantorial school, but none of them could sing as well as I could. The congregation was used to a singer from the Metropolitan Opera, so the fact that I could knock the socks off of the really dramatic repertoire was a big plus for me.

I sang a great audition. I knew I had done well. I was so *sure* that I got the job. But...I didn't get the job. I was devastated. This was my destiny...I knew it! I was used to being rejected, so I wasn't willing to take "no" for an answer. I had learned the value of "chutzpah" and wrote a letter to the President of the congregation saying that I had a feeling of destiny with that congregation and that I think they made the wrong choice. I invited them to call me when they discovered that to be true. Somehow, I knew I would get that call, and proceeded to follow my dream. I served a large congregation in Ohio the next Rosh Hashana and Yom Kippur as their Cantor. I was then accepted to sing a major leading role in one of my favorite operas in California, and had the pleasure of living with my mother for over three months, as we prepared and rehearsed for the opera. After opening night, I began to bleed and nothing would stop it but having a hysterectomy. That surgery was the end of any dream to get pregnant.

Nine months: the time it takes to create a baby in the womb. During those nine months following my audition for the congregation in New Jersey which I knew for a certainty would somehow someday be mine, I had been living my dream: singing and serving others.

Nine months after my first audition for the congregation in New Jersey, I got a call from the President: "Sheila...you were right...we did make a mistake...are you still available?" I got the job! I became cantor of a large congregation in New Jersey. As cantor, I would also be the one training the bar/bat mitzvah students. They wanted me to teach in the Hebrew School. A cantor in a big house, with lots of children. My dream—to live in a big house and have lots of children . . . As I was working hard preparing for my first Rosh Hashana and Yom Kippur services at my new congregation, I was undergoing radiation treatments for uterine cancer. While I was sweating and throwing up, I was also deliriously happy. My passion for my work gave me the strength to plow through the side effects of the treatments for my cancer. I knew in every cell of my body that I had found my pot of gold!

For over twenty years, I enjoyed using all my skills, talents, and my essential "me" as I taught in the school; created an academy of Jewish Studies for Teenagers; sang beautiful music; directed choirs, klezmer bands, and small classical instrumental ensembles; counseled individuals and families; and was considered by hundreds of congregants to be the "mother earth" of their community.

During my journey, life has been happening—not *to* me, but *for* me. That includes the bitter and the sweet, the agony and the ecstasy. While I never gave physical birth to any other child after Daedra, I've given emotional and spiritual birth to hundreds of children. Many men and women who have been congregants, clients, and friends have asked me to adopt them, feeling that I am in some way their "soul mother." Perhaps because I have learned to thrive in the face of surviving cancer, the deaths of children and other hardships, I can feel even more deeply the joy and gratitude of continuing to live my passion.

After retiring from serving my two congregations, I opened the doors to my office in Newburgh, where I've been living my new dream for over a decade. I had returned to school, receiving additional training for coaching and energy healing. As a Relationship and Life Transitions Coach, I work with individuals, couples, and families to build, create, and maintain loving relationships. Each day I pinch myself—I'm in heaven, living my dream every day of my life.

A few months after the passing of my beloved mother, I returned to my congregation in New Jersey for Yom Kippur—I wanted to honor my mother by saying Kaddish for her in the "big house" where I had been the "mother earth" my mother taught me to be. In the big house where I had shared my voice and my nurturing capacities with hundreds of families. As I was honoring my mother, I felt her with me on that day, as if she were holding my hand, saying "you see, honey, I knew you would live your dream!"

Yom Kippur 2013—My Legacy:

I walked into a familiar space: it was a space I had dedicated twenty-five years before that moment. It was a space I had filled with my voice, with music I had chosen, with voices I had trained, with musicians I had discovered and nurtured to play the music of the Jewish people. As I walked into the sanctuary which had been my home for thirteen years, I heard the organist playing the same melody I had introduced twenty-five years earlier. I saw the faces of people I had known for twenty-five years, children now grown with children of their own, people running over to greet and hug me. The familiar melody washed through me and around me, wrapping me in a warm blanket of nostalgia and legacy.

It was Yom Kippur—the holiest day of the Jewish calendar. I was a retired cantor, no longer singing during the holidays in any synagogue. I had come home to where I had begun my career as cantor, where I had first planted the seeds of melody—and I was hearing those same melodies twenty-five years later. The ushers had handed me a song booklet; as I looked closely, to my amazement, I realized it was the same booklet which I had compiled for my congregation. It was still being used. I knew it was from my hand, because the same typo I had made fifteen years earlier remained in that little booklet. Yes, it was from my hand.

As the service of Kol Nidre began, I began to feel the tears swelling up—first in my heart, then my throat, moving up to my eyes, then rolling down my cheeks. The congregation was still singing the melodies I had brought to them so many years ago! The musicians whom I had discovered like an excavator and a sleuth among the congregation's hidden treasures remained part of the musical fabric of my former congregation. The temple musician whom I had hired and trained to play with the "Jewish" style was still there, supporting the worship services.

At the conclusion of the beautiful Kol Nidre service, the Rabbi announced to the one thousand people assembled that their former cantor was with them. With that announcement, people looked for me, bringing me their grown children and grandchildren, crediting me with their love of Judaism and Jewish music. Couples whom I had married over the years came up to me with hugs and kisses, telling me stories of their children and hastening to let me know how everyone was thriving. It was as if I was at a family reunion and I was witnessing the growth and splendor of my very big family: children, grandchildren, and beyond; hearing tales of college, careers, marriages, and travel.

My heart was feeling very full. As I walked to my car that evening, the tears started to roll down my cheeks again. I actually had to pull over for a while, because it was difficult to see the road. I was having a "heart orgasm." I was feeling the accumulation of lived passion throughout my life. It was a wonderful feeling of that residual effect of all my work for so many years. I was basking in the light of feeling that I somehow mattered, and still do. I felt then—and feel now—those divine sparks tingling through my body and spirit.

As I closed my eyes that evening, I reminded myself of what I had learned in my early twenties and had been reminded of, repeatedly, throughout each challenge and adversity:

> *Life is not about time, it's about magic*
> *There are no guarantees*
> *Everything is on loan*
> *The only certainty is uncertainty . . . jump into the river . . . let*
> *go of the shore.*

Sheila's Lesson: Celebrating Challenges as Opportunities

How many people do you know who have overcome as many challenges as Sheila has and bless each one for the lessons learned? As I read Sheila's story, I felt like I traveled with her through many years of ups and downs. Sheila helps me to see the truth in her wise words that "the various circumstances of life have always been happening—not *to* me, but instead, *for* me."

Reflection

How could you view a challenging circumstance in your life as this experience happening *for* you? Imagine that your life is a movie and you are writing the script. How will you create your story? Will you succeed in transforming tragedies into opportunities, as you become the hero of your inspiring life?

The Gift of Gymnastics and Cheerleading: Mental and Physical Strength

Anna Blon

When I was a young girl, I was so shy that I would hide behind my mom and dad when people tried to talk to me. Once I was old enough to go into kindergarten, my parents decided that I should wait another year because I was so small and quiet. When I did enter school, I was able to make some friends, but it was always hard for me. After the first day of middle school, I remember coming home and hysterically crying because I had no friends. Insecure and scared, it was extremely difficult for me to step out of my comfort zone. Starting to do gymnastics was one of the most life-changing decisions that I have made. While I was rolling around on the gymnastics equipment in third grade, my gym teacher noticed some potential talent and suggested that I start taking classes. I began taking gymnastics at a place called the Little Gym and loved it. Learning new skills in gymnastics was fun and exciting, and helped me to be more outgoing.

After taking gymnastics for about a year, I came back to gym class in Maple Hill Elementary School and was the star of the class. Beating many boys in pull-ups and chin-ups made me feel very strong and confident. At Maple Hill, we received "stars" for completing a gymnastics move. I received stars for doing dips on the parallel bars, cartwheeling on the beam, doing a split on the beam, and doing a headstand, and I even earned one for doing an aerial. I have twenty stars—and have kept them in my room since elementary school.

After a couple years, I was too big for the Little Gym because my head would touch the ceiling if I jumped to the high bar. My parents found Sports, Fitness and Fun in Florida, New York, and signed me up for classes. During the first few classes, I was very nervous and scared. However, my coach, Michelle, was so supportive towards me, in a motherly way. She made me feel safe and comfortable learning to do new gymnastics moves. Learning how to do a back handspring was particularly exciting. One of the other coaches that I had during this time was especially helpful to me. Dan focused on having fun in gymnastics instead of being uptight and strict. His pep talks were supportive, and helped me to be more determined. Not only did I become more confident through gymnastics, I made a lot of new friends. Becoming friends with a group of girls meant so much to me; we had so much fun together. At the end of my eighth grade year, I qualified for a national competition held in Palm Springs, California.

After eighth grade, I decided that I would stop doing gymnastics and try to do cheerleading at my high school. During the football cheerleading tryouts, I was extremely nervous. It was really difficult for me to learn the sideline cheers and the dances. Cheerleading was about having straight arms and sharp movements, whereas gymnastics was focused on being graceful. Even though I was very nervous, there was a group of upperclassmen that really helped me out when I was struggling. I ended up making the JV team, which was very exciting for me. I became a "flyer," which was very nerve-wracking at first—flyers are the girls who are tossed up in the air during a routine.

My coach, Holly, was so supportive and positive; she really helped me to gain confidence in cheerleading. At first, I was very nervous and scared to be thrown in the air, but Holly always encouraged me and had faith in me. She saw potential in me and helped me to become a more confident athlete. To this day, she is an amazing role model for me. Toward the end of the football season, the varsity coach, Taylor, asked if I would like to move up to the varsity team. This was so exciting for me—the only freshman on the team. While cheering for varsity, I learned how to become a better flyer and cheerleader, and felt comfortable cheering for a crowd of people.

Cheerleading also helped me to become a tougher person; if I fell, I got right back up and kept trying. It was extremely exciting for me to be on the varsity team as a freshman, and it gave me so much more confidence. My teammates welcomed me with open arms, and accepted me as a new member of the team. So many of the upperclassmen took me under their wings and helped me to become more confident. Taylor pushed me to try new things, and encouraged me to try them again even if they didn't work out right away. She always made sure that I was improving, and doing the best that I could.

During my freshman year on the competition cheerleading team, I was the center point flyer for one of the stunt sequences. It made me feel extremely special to be the center of the routine. As a freshman, I looked up to the leaders on the team who were good role models and aspired to be like them. When cheerleading was very new to me, there were a few really supportive team members that helped me a great deal. I promised myself that I would help out the younger cheerleaders, in turn, to make sure that they would feel more confident and comfortable.

After cheerleading for a couple of years, I became a team leader and was grateful to have the opportunity to help other cheerleaders in the way that upperclassmen had helped me in the paSt As the seasons progressed, it was really great to watch these younger girls and guys gain skill and confidence the way I had. During my senior year, my basketball cheerleading coach, Kelly, helped me to become a better leader. She asked me if I would like to be team captain, and I was hesitant but very excited. However, Kelly helped me to overcome those fears and become a confident captain. She helped me to lead the team in a way that was successful, but not too pushy. Kelly was an extremely positive role model for me to have in high school, and she still is. She believed in my ability to lead the team, and I am so grateful for that. Being captain meant much more to me than having the title; it showed me that I could positively influence younger girls and guys. There have been a few younger cheerleaders that have come up to me and told me that I inspired them to try out for cheerleading, and that means more to me than they know.

I have become someone very different from that scared and shy little girl, and this is mostly due to gymnastics and cheerleading. Both sports helped me to be more comfortable with myself, and to be more outgoing when meeting new friends. I have met many new girls and guys who helped me to feel part of something special. Doing gymnastics and cheerleading helped me to not only be physically strong, but to become a stronger person mentally. Being a leader gave me the opportunity to see how important it is to me to help other people. My passion has not only become cheerleading, but also helping other cheerleaders to improve their confidence and sense of self while improving as an athlete. I now am much more confident, outgoing, and mature thanks to gymnastics, cheerleading, and all the great mentors who have helped me over the years.

Anna's Lesson: Building Strength and Confidence

Raising a child really does take a village. A steady progression of encouraging teachers, coaches and teammates have helped Anna build strength and confidence in herself. Gymnastics was a wonderful foundation for Anna, which she used to build her cheerleading career, where she has gained even more confidence to perform with a team, shout out cheers to a crowd and trust people to lift her high in the air.

Reflection

Most of us struggle with confidence in some area of our lives. Participating in sports is a great way to build both physical and mental strength, as you have learned from Anna's story. Gymnastics and cheerleading may not be the sports or activities for you, so take some time to experience activities that appeal to you.

Don't expect to be a pro when you first start. Watching a professional on TV is a lot different than playing yourself. Have fun and keep practicing. You may consider taking lessons or joining a group of people who enjoy being active.

GROWING INTO COMPASSION AND FORGIVENESS

Rev. Dechen Rheault

The First Passionate Step

Passion is a very interesting word with a meaning that permeates my being: a strong liking, deep interest, or devotion to some activity, object, or concept.

From the very beginning of my life, I believe I have lived from this place of great passion.

This was obvious to me even as I faced the decision to come into this world we call planet Earth. At some point, as a soul, I said, "Yes, I am ready now," and I prepared to enter into a physical realm. On December 8, 1950, I entered in Lawrence, Massachusetts, heading toward a life of great unknowns.

At birth, I was presented with this first great choice: to breathe or not to breathe? To manifest a physical body into the world requires this passionate, painful, glorious decision of all of us. Making that choice, I took my first deep breath.

And that's the beginning of a sixty-three-year journey of many passionate decisions, all leading back to the original choice of whether to be or not to be.

Survival in My World

On my birthday, I found myself in the arms of two Italians—one from Sicily, the other from Naples. We were a traditional Italian family living amongst—and surrounded by—grandparents, aunts, uncles, cousins, and other close family ties. And, of course, as family goes, we were traditionally dysfunctional. I became the caregiver or what some psychotherapist might call the "fixer" to everyone, trying to smooth out or "fix" any disruptions that may arise within the family. It did not take me long to extend that part of me into the neighborhood where kids often argued, fought, and were cruel to each other.

Every day of my childhood I made that decision to breathe . . . and then tried to figure out how I was going to do it that day. Would I survive if I did it wrong? What if I wasn't able to fix the problems in front of me? It always seemed to come down to survival for me . . . would my parents leave if the arguments were not fixed . . . would I have no friends if everyone stayed mad at each other? And so I lived a good part of those early years from an unconscious belief that my world would end if the people I cared about left or stopped caring. (No one did leave my world in the way I had feared. But I didn't see that until many years later, while in therapy dealing with the fear of loss and survival issues.)

As I grew up, I continued playing out my survival fears. One day, I found myself faced with what fear of survival really meant. I was eleven years old when I was kidnapped at knifepoint by a seventeen-year-old neighbor. Taken down into his dark, damp cellar, I left my body and only remembered my abductor's words: "If you tell anyone, I will lock you down in this dark cellar with the rats." Of course, I believed him and after I was released, kept that secret unconsciously locked away until I was in my thirties.

I was laying on a table receiving chiropractic bodywork when I had visions of the knife at my throat and my abductor's face. Then I remembered the entire incident, and was shaken to the core. While recalling and reliving the painful memory, I was faced with another important decisive moment: Do I breathe or not breathe? I breathed deeply and kept breathing as I made the decision to look closely at all of the parts of me that left that day. It was not easy, but necessary.

I did traditional therapy for a number of years as I discovered I was carrying trauma and post-traumatic stress, which was revealing itself in anxiety and panic attacks. The issues that surfaced were many: not feeling safe, feeling anger at my parents for not "protecting" me from my abductor, feeling guilt for not telling my parents, and feeling insecurity about what their reaction would have been. Would they have done something about it? Might they have blamed me for being at the abductor's house? I continued to have flashbacks to that time in my life and remembered how, around the time of the kidnapping, I would sit on a step in my yard, with a sharp rock in hand, and cut off the legs of ants. I was horrified as I remembered that scene and through therapy discovered it was my way of "getting back" at what had been done to me. To this day, I look at ants with great compassion and go out of my way to notice and protect them in any way I can.

I moved on to therapies that included mind/body therapies, breathwork, tapping, movement etc. These modalities helped me discover I was someone in a safe body that could go beyond the emotion and survival of that day.

Death and Rebirth

Many years before "reliving" those days, I had an opportunity to meet a "Holy" man who was visiting the United States. I was just in my twenties, and was invited to meet my good friend's teacher. She had often spoken about her teacher and the joy he had invoked in her. I was curious and cautious at the same time, but being someone who liked new experiences, I joined her for the occasion. I sat with a group of 100 students and newcomers as her teacher spoke of *shakti* and other words that meant little to me.

I found myself looking at the clock, hoping it would end soon. Finally, at what I thought was the end of the talk, I made my way to the door, as all the other attendees lined up to receive a blessing from him. Driving home that night, I wondered why I had decided to attend. I thought it was interesting, but not enough to understand why everyone was so excited about this teacher.

And then it happened . . . suddenly there was a flash of beautiful blue light filling the car. Instantly I found myself floating above the car, watching my body below driving at the steering wheel. For a moment I wondered if I had died, and my spirit had left my body. I was experiencing a most blissful state of being, where everything was one, and all cares slipped away. I can not say how long that moment lasted; however, at some point, I found myself turning into my driveway and walking into the house. My husband looked at me and asked if I was drugged, because I had a look on my face that mimicked a euphoric state.

It took a couple of days to come down from that experience. I noticed how I felt like a different person—more centered and peaceful. I called my friend and asked her who her teacher really was. I told her what had happened to me and that I wanted to understand the experience. She gave me more information about her teacher, his years of spiritual devotion, and his abilities to perform such *siddhis* when needed. I knew on the deepest level that there was a reason he provided me with such an experience and I wanted to know why.

This was the beginning of another large in-breath for me—this time into the life of Siddha Yoga with my teacher, Swami Muktananda. Through the years of sitting and meditating with him, I learned about the medicine and possibilities of miracles. It was a great time of growth for me, of breathing and blossoming. Daily I would feel and see the effects of his great love and abilities to open my heart and prepare me for the work I would eventually be doing, sparking a new passion . . .

It was a full moon night when Muktananda's aging body entered another realm.

I had just received the news from a dear friend. I was so saddened and had the need to be outside to grieve. While sitting on the grass in despair, I could hear his voice, as clear as though he were standing beside me. He told me to look up. When I followed his instruction, my gaze went directly to the full moon. In that moment, the moon changed its shape from round to a large, beautiful lotus flower. On one level, I could not believe what I was seeing; however, knowing his great power and special abilities, I knew what I was seeing was a final gift from him, reminding me that there are no boundaries of time and space and all things are possible. Even so, for several months, I grieved the loss of my dear teacher.

Dealing with Grief

Grief is such a difficult emotion to be with. During grief, everything around me begins to feel surreal. With the loss of family, friends, clients and animals, I find myself on a great roller coaster of emotions. In some cases, the anxiety and panic returns, forcing me to look at survival and fear over and over. Sometimes, during the process of grieving, visions of past lives where I died in unfavorable conditions would arise.

Each of these was another chance to take a deep breath in. I chose to put myself in the middle of the issues of dying and loss by working with the dying and being present at the passing of those I care about. I indulged myself in learning about the dying process through studying different religions and their beliefs of death and rebirth.

Death and Rebirth on Another Level

Raising my two children alone gave me the opportunity to experience death and rebirth in a different way. I was challenged daily and questioned my ability to be a good mom. I didn't truly know what a "good mom" was supposed to look like, but I was sure I wasn't meeting the criteria. My patience was tested regularly. Sometimes I passed with flying colors, other times—I found out later, rather than sooner—my words were painful to their innocent ears.

When my son became a teenager, I saw him developing habits that weren't healthy for him. I began to set rules and boundaries which he tested and rejected regularly. It was when he physically threatened me that we entered into family therapy. His resistance to this grew and he continued to act out. When he was sixteen, he quit school and made it clear he was not going back. I felt great despair, feeling alone and not knowing what to do.

Finally, I took the extreme route and applied tough love. I let him know he would have to follow the house rules, or leave. He left.

What's a Mother to Do?

There are no words to describe the feeling inside when a child leaves at the age of sixteen and a half. He had no money, food, or place to go. I called my friends for support and was advised to let him go, believing he would see that house rules don't compare to living on the streets. He was gone for a week when a friend of mine told me she had seen him in the city, twenty minutes from our home. I got in my car and went looking for him. When I found him, he was hanging out with friends and looking a little shabby. He told me he was staying at a friend's apartment in Burlington. I asked him to show me where, and gave him money for food.

I visited my son a couple of times a week, bringing him provisions and monitoring his activities. He seemed happy to see me, and content with his living situation.

Then, two months after his move out of the house, I got a call from him saying he was going to kill himself—he had nothing to live for and wanted to end it. I could feel my insides turning cold. I couldn't think, act, or move. All that went through my mind was "What do I do? How can I reach him?"

I took a deep breath and called my male friends from the spiritual community I was involved in. Five of those men went to my son's side and sat with him through the night, sharing stories of what it had been like for them, going through tough times in their teenage years.

My son did not return home. He met a woman who helped change his life. He got his GED, took college courses, apprenticed and worked with an antique dealer, and learned the trade of repair and refinishing antiques—and, now, has a reputable business nearby.

Through those years of testing, in the uncertainty of decisions to be made as a parent, I took a very deep breath in, remembering that anything is possible, loving both of my children passionately and unconditionally. After that, friends and acquaintances would often hear me say, "If you can raise children, you can do anything."

The Work I Choose

As years passed, the children became young adults, and chose their professions; one as a woodworker, the other an environmental biologist. My passions, however, lay in service work of a different nature.

From the time I was a child, I found myself surrounded by elders. I lived in the same house with my maternal grandfather and paternal grandparents. There was no room to avoid their needs as they aged and I seemed to be a willing helper. It began with one grandfather asking for a regular back scratch and his daily coffee. As years passed, the care increased as well as my awareness of their every need in their fragile states.

It was when I was raising my children alone and looking for another part-time job that I felt drawn to caregiving for the elderly. I started off as a home-health aide for the Visiting Nurse Association and, a year later, found myself as the cook and caregiver for the Vanderbilt family. I cared for them many years until their passing. Through my reputation, I was soon sought out by many affluent families to give care to their family members. As another chapter passed, I was invited to be a co-owner of an elderly care home that offered alternative healing, healthy food, and creative activities.

During these years of caregiving jobs, I continued the work as a part-time massage therapist that I had trained for in my twenties and thirties. In fact, my passion to continue my studies in alternative healing and spiritual modalities never stopped. I studied Reiki, Shiatsu, and Polarity, and established a Reiki school and clinic in the local area. I also continued my study and practice with the spiritual teachers of the Cherokee, Hindi, and Buddhist traditions that I had first explored in my younger years.

Through all these lifelong experiences, I found my senses becoming very acute. I could see, feel, hear, smell, and experience life in a more sensitive way, and I found teachers who could help me fine-tune and enhance what I was experiencing from these awakened senses. It was through these studies that I took another deep breath in. I made the passionate decision to step into a ministry whereby I would make myself available for the care and healing of our precious earth and all beings in this and all realms.

The Greatest Lesson

One of my Buddhist teachers, Garchen Rinpoche, came into my life about twenty years ago. He had just recently been released from a Chinese prison, where he had been tortured for twenty-seven years. I sat with him in great wonderment over his compassionate nature and ability to forgive all those who hurt him. He told us, according to his spiritual belief, that what he experienced as a prisoner was his karma. His tradition taught him about compassion and, while in prison, he showed joy and compassion towards his torturers. Through his ability to hold them in this way, their ways began to change. The soldiers began to care about him and show their own compassion toward him. This lesson taught me much about forgiving those who have hurt me throughout my life. I have tested this great lesson of forgiveness and found that those whom I have forgiven and have compassion toward seem to walk a little gentler on the earth.

When I look back on my life, I sense that from the very beginning my soul aligned to the path I chose, even before I passed through my mother's body. I believe we enter here on earth for our soul's journey into the great state of enlightenment. For each of us, the journey will take different turns. The people we meet along the way help us to feel and learn the most valuable lessons on our own unique paths. Of all these lessons, living with compassion for all beings, no matter what the circumstance, stands out for me. This is what truly sparks my passion.

Dechen's Lesson: Compassion for Myself and All Beings

Dechen did the best that she could as a young child. The trauma from a horrible incident was trapped inside her, until she was receiving bodywork one day and that scary event came back into her consciousness. Her body had helped her by holding onto this memory until she was ready to heal and process what happened.

Dechen continued to learn and practice a variety of modalities to help her heal. As she has healed and learned from spiritual masters, such richness has come into her life. Each challenge has given Dechen the opportunity to learn more spiritual mastery at deeper levels, learning to be compassionate toward herself and all beings. How lucky I feel to be learning from the wisdom Dechen shares with us.

Reflection

Do you have traumatic experiences that have happened in your life? What healing modalities have you explored? Remember that one form of healing may help you clear one level and then it might be time to use another method for a different level. Each person is unique, so pay attention to what works and doesn't work for you. Enjoy the words from this SPARKS Inspiration card:

Hope!

I have noticed that when I feel overwhelmed, I think that I am the only person in the world that feels this way. When I share my situation with a positive person,
I discover that they can relate to me. This makes me feel relieved and hopeful.

Healing:

Find a person who will listen to me with compassion and share my story.

Affirmation:

I feel safe to share and be me.
~ Maria Blon & Ann Bell

FROM FOGGY EXISTENCE TO BRIGHT LIVING

Brian K. Baird

A profound awareness has come to me in recent years: although I have some skills and talents, "smartness" has largely eluded me. I didn't always feel that way, but an honest, deep assessment makes it pretty clear. It's not that I am a complete idiot, but if you could score my navigation of life's experiences on a spectrum of intelligence, I'd be pretty far from brilliant. And in this deeper examination of my life, it's also pretty obvious to me that my consciousness has been enveloped in a fog, blocking efforts at learning and communication. I find it more glaring when I meet or experience the work of really intelligent people and get the opportunity to see how their minds work. *No fog.* It fills me with awe and a wee bit of envy.

What's caused my fogginess? Perhaps it's hereditary. My father, long deceased, and my brother have embodied many definitions of mental illness. Perhaps some mental challenges have trickled into my system (perhaps a lot . . . who knows). My father gallivanted much of the time and was rarely around, home just enough to tease me with desire for time with him. Perhaps I learned to mute my feelings, where feelings might be an important part of our liveliness and clarity. My parents divorced the summer before my ninth birthday and my mother, brother, and I moved in with my grandmother and alcoholic grandfather—a man who had long forgotten what it was like to be a child and did not tolerate children. Perhaps I wrapped myself in an emotional cocoon. Whatever the cause, it seems to me that fogginess served me in my youth. I may have been quite a bit aimless, but when I made bad choices, they were rarely physically harmful ones—no drugs or alcohol for me. I was already emotionally and intellectually insulated and didn't need to self-medicate. My mother, though well meaning, had so much work to do on herself that she was not available to me. I learned early on to rely on myself for comfort and advice, and I wasn't up for this task. I was unable to manage the decline in self-esteem that accompanied these ugly times; an effect that was only compounded as I made one mistake and ugly choice after another. Perhaps some choices were so I'd feel *SOMETHING* through the fog. I liberated small things from other people; I stole things. I got into lots of fights, even if I knew I was going to be the loser. Eventually, and accordingly, I became a loner.

I never felt sorry for myself, not then, not now. I just plodded along without direction or recourse or awareness of what was going on with me and around me. At some unconscious level, I have always known I had such handicaps, especially in social settings, but it is only recently that I have become openly alert and aware to them. Despite all of these issues and attributes—and with only a few distinct events in my life to note as exceptions—somehow I've developed a shrug-it-off sense of optimism that things would one day work out. In my view, this has served me well. My closest friend has described my style as "HUMAS": Head Up My Ass Syndrome. Countless times where the world could be falling down around me, I would look at things through optimistic lenses, even a happiness filter, that has often unsettled those close to me. It often looked like I didn't care, when in reality I was just living in that foggy, muted world inside my head. The caution flag with this kind of existence is that when emotion did make it to the surface, it was often rage.

My assessment isn't strictly my own, by the way. In high school, I had more than one teacher—and even a guidance counselor—who made it clear I should consider a vocation rather than college. They said in supportive and compassionate tones that I "simply didn't have what it takes" to make it through college. Because of focus issues, discipline issues, aimlessness, and a limited sense of self-esteem, I accepted their accounting.

You might think that low self-esteem is incompatible with optimism. I operated in such a thought-stopping cloud that I didn't focus on anything and just plodded along as if nothing was wrong. Yet, when you blend this unrealistic positivity with elusive intelligence and low confidence—and a bit of aimlessness—things could go a number of ways. I often would go for long walks (perhaps you could call these gallivanting moments), and one day I found myself in a neighboring town on Long Island and, on impulse, walked into a US Navy recruiting office. Other than the hurdle of a later-provided parental signature (I was only seventeen, and my mother acquiesced, despite concerns), and finishing high school, I enlisted on the spot. I was inducted that summer.

There was an exam administered during that first visit to the recruiting office to help me evaluate possible roles. Between the results and the recruiter's goals, I opted to join the Naval Nuclear Propulsion Program. I was going into the nuclear power business. The recruiter, in a supportive and compassionate tone, convinced me I had a good chance of succeeding in the program and, even if I didn't, the rapid rank advancement for those in the program would give me a head start wherever else I landed in the Navy. I wasn't fretting about my chances of success at the time, but the built-in Plan B was a nice plus.

The first months in the Navy were boot camp in thunderstorm-ridden central Florida, during which I turned eighteen, followed by training in my core discipline in freezing cold Great Lakes, Illinois. Because of the built-in rewards for being in the program, I entered Nuclear Power preschool in Orlando having been already elevated by four enlisted ranks after less than five months in the Navy. So far, though, I was only a steam plant mechanic. It was pretty straightforward and unambitious to march in step, shoot an M1 rifle (three shots, one time), and study how to repack a valve or control the flow of steam to a turbine generating electricity. I didn't really have to think, only absorb some logical information. But plodding along with my cloudy head and foggy thinking wasn't going to help me through the next stages of my naval experience.

Nuke Power Preschool, back in thunderstorm country, was where the Navy weeded out those who weren't cut out for the core of the program, while giving the survivors the basics they would need to succeed. Though I've always had an interest in science, the basic physics was pretty rough and tough, and I found the math to be quite defeating. I just wasn't getting it. I wasn't cutting it. With only two weeks left in

"Preschool," my grades were horrible (especially in math where I hadn't passed one exam), and prospects for continuing with the program were dismal. I began asking myself what to do. I could either give up or double my efforts. Should I continue trying, or quit and take it easy? After all, I had Plan B, and there was such little time to pull myself out of the hole. I didn't have any serious experience with success and I had numerous moments of failure, which I accepted with my unique, cloudy optimism. I had a sense, however, that this was a pivotal point that I needed to look at more closely. I took a long walk, not gallivanting this time, ending up at Church Street Station, miles from the naval training center.

It wasn't so apparent to me at the time, but I can recall the feelings now, and I was profoundly unhappy. I had a strong distaste for the structure and accountability of the Navy. I wasn't particularly good with authority, which should have scared me if I was more aware and more intelligent. Despite the unhappiness, perhaps because of it, all of my thoughts were compellingly clear: no fog. I had to make a decision about my next steps. Every person I could think of to reach out to for advice had been judgmental with me in the past and I would not expose myself to new attacks. It felt, to me, that once again I could only count on myself, and be my own council. There were voices in my head that may have been mine, or perhaps the vestiges of positive voices in the past, perhaps angels. I don't know. Wherever they were from, in that moment of clarity I realized I had to break from aimless meandering—impulse-created and accidental—and form a goal, a destiny, a place I wanted to be. I realized that Plan B was still an option, but I would exercise that later if needed. I did not know how things were going to finish and I lacked the certainty of confidence, but I was resolved to focus without distraction on passing math and physics and continuing on in the Nuke Power Program.

The decision turned out to be the easy part. The decision was the fuel for action. But the task, with limited time to complete, was the most massive of challenges. Moving forward was slow, all uphill, and I did not know what to do. It turned out that with a little extra effort and tweaking, plus my new resolve, the physics would be passable; it was the math that seemed far out of my grasp and abilities. A young ensign, whose name I have shamefully forgotten (that fog thing, remember), who was teaching the math curriculum was conducting after-class work for those who needed it. I went to every session. I stopped socializing. I practiced the math problems, though I rarely understood the underpinnings of what I was doing. I worked even harder on the math, staying up into the wee hours, irritating my roommates because I had nowhere to go to study, trying to teach my brain to use the logic that had eluded me. With each quiz, I still failed. With each day, I was increasingly disheartened that I just couldn't get over the hump. The young ensign was encouraging, though he, too, told me in that supportive and compassionate tone I had heard before that there were worse things than failing out of the Nuke Power Program. Perhaps he just wanted to soften the blow.

There were glimmers of insight that happened from time to time. I remember the excitement of the ensign, his eyes popping wide open, his face turning red, contrasting with his Navy khakis, but then the logic would evaporate with a "Poof" into my cloudy brain, and I would still find success just out of reach. There were, however, small—but noticeable—improvements in my understanding. The question came down to whether I was going to be able to do enough to make a difference. All that was left was the comprehensive exam and a few short days.

There were no classes for three days before the final. I was so intent on studying that I didn't eat for the first two days. The pressure was tremendous. And then the sound of a loud, electric guitar came wafting through the walls from a neighboring unit in the dorms. I couldn't function. I couldn't think. The cloudy brain was slowing me down at every step. And now this intrusion on my thinking. Angrily I went next door and ORDERED him to shut that thing off. When he proceeded to slam the door in my face and continue to crank out the sounds of Rush (he was a pretty good guitarist, by the way . . . it just didn't matter at the time), I stormed out onto the walkway outside of our dorms and, as I passed his room, I put my fist through the glass of his unit's very large window. The noise of shattering glass was satisfying and he abruptly stopped playing guitar to get out of the way of the exploding glass shards. It felt great to win that battle. But, quite quickly—again with clarity that had often eluded me—I realized I had done myself harm in the process. What were the ramifications? I did not know.

I decided to turn myself into the base MPs before super-guitarist could do so, trying to get ahead of the ugly thing I had created. There were no cell phones or room phones then, and it was a significant march to the MPs. Along the way, I became aware that the sounds of glass shattering can be heard at great distances because I was being praised and congratulated by other studiers for halting the disruptive music. Nevertheless, I stepped continuously along the way without acknowledging them, marching—to what level of doom, I did not know. I was deeply consumed by my concern—in a daze, if you will, if not my usual fog—that I had altered my path because of what was later labeled as "wanton destruction of government property."

The MPs were not kind, but also not hard. They matter-of-factly took my report and while they were awaiting an over-the-phone adjudication from a JAG officer, I sat in the brig, door opened and unlocked. I did get fed, though—my first meaningful food in a couple of days—which emotionally softened the situation. It was hours later before I signed documents that stated that the government would garnish my paycheck to pay for the window repair and that also included a warning that would go in my record.

Somehow, in my absence, I had become legend. Upon returning to my dorm room, the only place I could go so I could continue to prepare for my math final, there were dozens of people milling around, all wondering if I was ever going to return. Applause. Cheers. Wide-eyed amazement at the story. In hindsight, perhaps the broken window wasn't such a horrible crime, even though it was an act committed in rage, but I felt horrible, that I had let myself down. There was a plus, though: we never heard that guitar again.

The next day. I took the physics final and continued studying the math. I visited the ensign one more time, perhaps looking for sympathy and an escape option. We worked on the problems I brought to him, but he eventually kicked me out of his office so he could go home to his family, using a supportive and compassionate tone, saying that "all will work out as intended."

Throughout the evening, my textbook was open. I looked at my workbook and notes. But I was staring past the material. I was still resolved to finish with my best effort, but I was exhausted and further dazed. That night, as I tried to sleep, what little sleep time I did have was dramatized, if not traumatized, by unsolvable math problems where the geometry, numbers, and formulas were brilliantly colored in neon lighting and moving in and out of view with all kinds of shrinking, enlarging, and sliding by. I woke up sleep deprived, but less exhausted, even a bit charged up. The test was three hours long, starting at 0900 hours. The problems passed in and out of my view, almost like in my dream. I wrapped up exactly at the "time's up" point and went with my classmates to lunch, after which we'd return to get our grades. When asked how I did, I simply said, "I don't know. I hope I passed." If I passed the comprehensive test, I would automatically get a review to see if I could continue. If I failed, there would be no review and I did not know where I was going to land.

It seems to me that anticipation is the biggest way to slow down our time experience, and lunchtime took FOREVER. I simply wanted to get the results over with and begin new plans if needed. As we sat in the classroom afterward and the tests were being handed out, the ensign was calling out students' names and their scores, something he'd never done before. The good grades were called first, and those students with the good grades were not a surprise. They always seemed to be on firm ground with this subject. As the names and grades continued to be announced, the grades were getting lower. And I wasn't being called. Now I was in dread of not only failing, but having the whole world know. Finally, all of the other tests were handed out but mine. Everyone had passed so far. And then I had insight into what the ensign was going to do. He was going to give me my test score in private. Or so I thought. He started talking about the continuum of learning and the true meaning of passing and failing and how we should learn from all of our experiences and so on and so on. I was becoming horrified that I was going to be some kind of example for how *not* to be or for how to accept our lot in life or whatever else he was going to announce. He then noted how I'd struggled, how I'd been in every extra session with him for the last two weeks, how I had shown dogged determination despite continuing challenges with the material. I couldn't fathom where he was going with this and my dread increased. I didn't think of this man as being so cruel, but I was certain I was being laid open before all to satisfy a hidden, twisted, dark compulsion. And with the heightened dread came heightened clarity. To this day, that moment is crystal clear and part of a huge pivotal moment as he announced that I had the highest score on the exam, missing only one point, earning a 3.96. Our ENTIRE class had passed and I was certainly continuing with the program. I was amazed. I was relieved. I was invigorated. And though there's a part of me that doesn't feel deserving of anything good that happens, I felt deserving. I felt deserving because of my hard work, even though I wasn't so sure about deserving the best test score (because of the fog, considering I was concerned about merely passing, I still don't know how I could have done so well without knowing it).

The preschool version of the Nuke Power Program was the first weeding, and I had passed. And when they formed the twelve classes that would be part of the next stage core academic program, they were sorted by likelihood of succeeding. If you were in section one, it was pretty much a lock that you had what it takes to finish, and finish well. If you were in section twelve, the failure and drop-out rates were expected to be very high. I was put into section five, which gave me a confidence boost about my future in the Navy AND Nuclear Power. If they believed in me enough to put me in section five, I could do it. Combining that with the unbelievable finish in preschool, my self confidence really skipped upward a notch or two. And I became an avid student of Nuclear Power, finishing second in my section, and not too far from the top of the entire class (I don't remember exactly, but something like twenty-third out of 600). I had determined, more than anything else, that if I put my mind to something, I could accomplish it. Make a decision, get into action, and go to the finish. This became my code.

So, you might think that you've heard enough, that you get my point that we can do anything we set our minds to. And, to a degree, that's been the aim. But there's a bit more to this.

You see, I have been blessed throughout my life and I am most grateful for my successes. In the thirty-plus years since my days in the Navy and the Nuclear Propulsion Training Program (which I finished),

I went on to college and got a degree in computer science with minors in engineering and MATH. I've worked for a division of a Fortune 50 company, owned my own company several times, embarked on a path of personal discovery in my relationship with sales, married a beautiful woman, moved into a wonderful home, and adopted a brilliant (unfogged), stunningly beautiful little girl from China. In my most recent days in corporate America, I was the top producer for most of my twelve years with a start-up company in Silicon Valley.

With each of these events and successes, I gained the experience and additional confidence to do the next thing. And I often detailed to others that success started with a decision. How could the message be any different than making a decision, taking action, and finishing? But then there's the human side of this. The framework for success, which is hugely fostered by developing your confidence, can bend in ugly ways if it is not managed properly. If you don't start out with a sense of humility and maintain it, and you continue to experience success, it can lead to feelings of infallibility, which is the glue of arrogance. In my case, arrogance was compounded by the fact that I had always been my own council, never having had a mentor. So I never sought or accepted any advice or ideas that were not originated by me. That hubris created a pretty massive fall.

In recent years, as I noted, I was the biggest producer at a start-up company in Silicon Valley. New leadership was inserted into the company when I had been at the company for over ten years, and this new leadership defined a need to drive the whole company to greater success which, instead of replicating methods that were working for me, involved going in directions which I vehemently disagreed with. I made it two more years before being "involuntarily separated." It was then that I began the struggle to find a new place to channel my energy.

It's been more than three years since I was fired, and I decided then that I was going to stop focusing on myself and, instead, to help others. I had learned so much, how could I not make a difference in other people's lives by sharing my successes? I started writing books—one on sales, the other on the ethics of business. But, as one can imagine, it's not too hard to see that I was full of hubris and could not be told anything. No advice.

No council. My way was the correct way. Everything else was wrong. Everything suffered when I couldn't accept help, when my ego lacked empathy because I was wrapped in layers of success and arrogance. My marriage suffered. My relationships with friends were neglected. My confidence was shaken to the core. How could I possibly help people if I didn't know how to accept help myself? How could I show people how to succeed, if the finished product lacked humility and damaged important relationships? I had to shelve EVERYTHING, and rethink, rebuild.

I haven't lost sight of my desire to help other people. My paramount goal, my prime directive, is to help others. But I am in the process of redefining what success means so that it doesn't destroy people and their relationships in the process. Along the way, I hope to save my marriage, continually discover new messages and meanings to life—my life for sure—and really begin truly helping change the world in bright, effective, meaningful ways. So, with the lessons of recent times, added to those lessons from the rest of my years, I aim to be a better person and successful in the right way. Make a decision, take APPROPRIATE action, and go to the finish. The same idea, supported by new lessons. Though smartness is sometimes still elusive, and the cloud isn't really gone, there is clarity in becoming more deeply aware of my strengths and weaknesses, especially when blended with confidence and humility. Through being deflated and ultimately humbled from my fall, I have discovered the embrace of humility and its power. Whenever arrogance isn't leaping out from behind bushes and building corners to admonish my ego for being so idle, I find I have the power to understand people in compassionate ways that had been hidden from me before. This enables me to truly help others (most of the time; I still make lots of mistakes, some to make you laugh, others to make you cry). But, as it gets easier to operate without it being all about me, I recognize a new and very important meaning of success.

Like the phoenix from the ashes, I have transformed one of my biggest failures, certainly my biggest fall, into something far more relevant that enables me to truly help others. I also have clarity of purpose, though with fuzziness about methodology. I have found tremendous enthusiasm and passion for what's to come and, with that, even greater clarity is poking through. No matter how little sleep I've gotten (and I've not gotten a lot, lately), I have no problems getting up and working on my mission to help others. You might call it a passion for purpose, a new meaning for success. I find that quite invigorating.

Brian's Lesson: Helping People with Humility

My heart breaks with tenderness when I think of Brian's courage in telling his sometimes painful story with humor, honesty, and humility. How many children feel alone growing up, without loving guidance to soften the blows that they experience? Brian did the best that he could by creating his plan for moving forward. While his outcome was not always pretty, he learned from his mistakes, kept going and was very successful in the business world. Brian reflected on how his actions effect the people around him. Now Brian's focus is taking the emphasis away from himself and finding ways to help people. He has a newfound passion and purpose in life. Life is exciting and meaningful to Brian like never before. I admire Brian's courage to share his story while he is still in the process of getting more clarity about exactly what his mission is.

Reflection

I imagine that you may be feeling like Brian, that something isn't right about the way that you are living. Unraveling what changes you would like to make takes time. Brian is getting closer, but is not there yet. Know that it is okay to not know, to be in a space of being open to possibilities, allowing for new ways of living to come into your life. When you have clarity about what direction you want to head in your life, try Brian's method:

- Make a decision,
- Take APPROPRIATE action, and
- Go to the finish.

LITTLE MAN WITH A BIG HEART
Jean Widletson Gaspard

The original reason for interviewing eight year old Jean Widletson Gaspard was for a children's book comparing the day in the life of a child in Merger, Haiti, at the HEART School, with a child at the Truman Moon School in Middletown, New York. I never expected to receive so much wisdom and compassion from a young boy.

I was able to put together the following story about Gaspard using interviews with his teacher Magdala Jean Baptist, HEART School Director of Operations Shad St Louis, Community Liaison Carina Blon, and School Director Dieumaitre Derosie. It was made possible with translation help from Shad and Carina.

Home and Family

While his given name is Jean Widletson Gaspard, he goes by Gaspard, pronounced "Gaspa," with the "r" and "d" silent. Gaspard lives in a rented cinder block house filled with only necessities, bordered by gardens of sugar cane, plantains, and mango trees. He lives with his mother and two brothers, who are both younger than him. He sleeps in a bed with one brother, while the baby is in his mom's bed. They have an outhouse and a well on the property—simple luxuries in a third world country. Gaspard's father never comes to the house. Sometimes, the family sees him in the street working. When asked about his father, Gaspard says, "My father has a motorcycle and can build big houses."

Gaspard has a little garden. He noticed that, when he waters his garden, the plants grow. When he doesn't water, the plants don't do well. Gaspard told us, "I had to teach my brother not to take the tops off the plants. I got mad when he did that and stopped watering. Now I am watering again, and the plants are growing."

School

Gaspard walks more than a mile to school, where he attends second grade—which he is repeating due to difficulty with reading. My husband Tom, my friend Anthony, Gaspard's classmate Danielo and I walked with Gaspard to school on Monday, January 6, 2014. He was eagerly waiting for us at 6:30 am. Anthony took pictures, then Gaspard took Anthony's very heavy camera bag and carried it to school, in addition to his already-heavy book bag. Gaspard had a bounce in his step the whole thirty-six-minute, more than a mile, walk to school.

Gaspard's favorite subjects are math, writing, English, and drawing. He is very talkative and loves to play soccer and other games with his friends at recess. He says he would always like to go to school and will work hard. Gaspard is very kind. He enjoys walking the preschoolers to lunch, holding their hands and gently leading them to the cafeteria.

Gaspard's biggest challenge in school is reading. His mother is not involved in his learning. Gaspard studies by himself, but needs someone to give him more attention and help. School Director Dieumaitre discussed getting a reading circle organized to help Gaspard and other students at the school who need tutoring. Shad and third grade teacher Magdala Jean Baptiste have organized the third grade students to tutor the younger children after school. This additional learning time for motivated children without home support will be invaluable.

Gaspard's Mother

Gaspard helps his mom by getting water when she washes clothes, because she can't carry the water buckets. He also goes shopping for her since she can't walk well. In fact, at the time of our visit (on January 6, 2014), Gaspard's mother had an infection in her leg which had been hurting for almost two weeks, and a large boil had erupted behind her knee which was oozing with blood and fluid. She had a cloth to catch what came out and said that she could not afford to go to the doctor.

Through Carina, we found out that the clinic was open the next day, and she could see the doctor for the equivalent of six dollars, American. Anthony gave her more than enough to cover her visit to the clinic. When we saw Gaspard a few days later, we asked how his mother was doing. He explained that she could not walk to the doctor, so did not go for help, and her leg was still very painful. I felt frustrated that getting medical attention for his mom was so challenging. I worried about her, hoping that she would get better soon. By the end of January, her leg was better and she was able to attend a conference with Gaspard's teacher Magdala. It was one more example of how a medical problem which is simple to fix here in the States is much more challenging in Haiti. Gaspard told us that he would like to be a doctor so that he can help his mom and other people when they are sick. He also likes learning about how plants can help people heal. Gaspard has never been very sick himself. He told us that, a few times, he just threw up, but that was all.

When we asked him about his life, Gaspard told us his favorite food is rice with bean sauce or vegetable sauce. Through our interpreters, we asked him a few more questions, which are asked and answered, below:

What is the best part of your life, Gaspard?

- I love my mom.
- I love life.
- I love school, because they make an effort for me.
- I like when I have work to do, like carrying water for my mom to use. When I have constructive things to do, I feel lighter.
- I like to help other kids with their homework.
- What is the worst part of your life?
- I don't like when kids fight.
- I don't like when my mother or brothers are suffering. I feel scared for them.

After we asked our questions, Carina asked if Gaspard had any questions for us. Gaspard asked if we live well in the States, then asked what our parent's names are and where they live. Then he started talking more, saying, "Here, people don't put their heads together and work as a team. When I get older, I want to put my head together with people and work as a team to make this country better. If people put their heads together, this country would be rich."

We thought we were finished, but Gaspard said, "You didn't ask me what kinds of trees I like." And then he began to tell us that he likes trees with fruit that make people better. He asked me what kinds of trees I like, and I said that I like mango trees. Gaspard asked what kind, because there are many different kinds of mangoes.

Gaspard also explained that there are many trees that you just "put a leaf on you and you heal." His mom said that papaya trees are healing trees. Gaspard learned in school that there are trees in the States that do not grow in Haiti, and trees in Haiti that do not grow in the States. He asked if we could send him seeds to grow one of our trees in Haiti, but I explained that in New York it is very cold with snow and ice. The trees from there would not grow in Haiti. Gaspard said that he would put a big chunk of ice next to the tree, and another one on top of the tree, each morning before school so the tree would be cold. When the tree was big, he would send it to us to grow but he was not sure there would be a train big enough.

Gaspard told us that he had heard about trains. He would like to see trains and wants to see people "put their heads together." Gaspard doesn't like when aid workers in Haiti give out food and fighting breaks out. If he was giving out food, he would share and bring things to people's houses. I asked if he would like a picture of trees in New York. He said if we could send one, he would like a picture—or we could get part of a tree and send it to him. He and his mom were all smiles as we said goodbye. We were almost to Shad's house—about a ten-minute walk away—and Gaspard came running to us and said, "A word I have to say; I love you all with all my heart."

The next day, with Carina's help translating, we asked Rosita, the neighborhood herbal expert, if she would teach Gaspard what plants to use to help in the healing of his mom's leg. So Rosita asked Gaspard to arrive at school early and she would teach him when she made tea in the morning, which he did.

I hope that Gaspard continues to learn from Rosita. I love helping people to connect and learn from each other.

Gaspard's Lesson: Hope through Wisdom and Action

Gaspard is such a gentle, kind, and thoughtful young boy wise beyond his years, despite living in great poverty. My hope is that he will be able to keep going to school, and to study in the medical field while learning about plant remedies, which can be helpful to his people. I imagine Gaspard inspiring people in Haiti to "put their heads together" and work as a team to make their country better. I know that he will be leading people with his heart.

Here is a quote from a world leader who shares Gaspard's philosophy of hope and doing good:

The best way to not feel hopeless is to get up and do something. Don't wait for good things to happen to you. If you go out and make some good things happen, you will fill the world with hope, you will fill yourself with hope. ~ Barack Obama

Reflection

Children often have wisdom beyond their years that could inspire adults to see situations from a fresh and hopeful perspective. Have you ever tried listening to a child's ideas about how to make the world better? Resist the urge to correct their thinking. Listen fully, engage in their stories, and allow them to take you away to a place of innocence that you may not have visited for some time.

Give yourself a vacation by listening to a child and playing with a child. Immerse yourself in his or her world and see what happens. Then, as an adult, consider what action you could take to help make dreams of a world filled with hope a reality.

A Constant Wind Keeps Pushing Me Forward.

Anthony Church

For as long as I can remember, there has been a constant wind behind my back that keeps pushing me forward—sometimes gusting and other times blowing gently, but never ceasing. That wind is generated by a fire of desire for something greater, something bigger, something better. There have been notable periods in my life when that fire has raged like a roaring hell-bent inferno, balanced by times where it burns evenly and steadily like a large dense piece of firewood. So why would someone so driven by desire be writing about finding his passion? In this way, I am in a different dimension of the paradigm of passion. I do not wander through life trying to find what interests me. In fact, my interests are many and varied. It has been so long since I've felt boredom that I very honestly have forgotten what it feels like. Instead, the opposite is true. Almost every element of human existence has my interest. For someone with such a strong drive to act on his interests, this has been both a blessing and a curse. And this is where my journey to find my true ultimate passion begins: in the weeds of a strong and vast open field of interests and a desire to experience an innumerable variety of the many opportunities and experiences life has to offer.

This trait has played itself out in many different ways in my life. By the age of twenty-three, despite growing up with a serious lack of resources and without much opportunity to pursue self-actualization, I had already experienced a lot. Much of my desire manifested itself in entrepreneurial endeavors—starting at the age of seven. Understanding the concept of profit for the first time, I would secure some candy—mostly Blow Pops—in bulk and sell it on the school bus. If I paid ten cents for a piece of candy off the bus, and sold it for twenty-five cents on the bus, I could make fifteen cents per sale. I didn't necessarily have the math skills to be able to calculate profit, but I knew I had more at the end than I did at the beginning. Between then and the age of twelve, I set up many classic lemonade stands and held garage sales (I always sold for way too low). In my entrepreneurial zeal, I decided to use my garage sales to generate more revenue by setting up games that could be played in which, I thought, the odds were in my favor. The games would cost ten cents or so to play and, if the players won, they could select from one of several garage sale item prizes. I ended this practice after being repeatedly outsmarted by older neighborhood kids and learning some valuable lessons.

At the age of twelve, I decided to exercise my entrepreneurial muscle in a slightly more traditional method. I started my first "business," which I called A&V Residential. It was really nothing more than some flyers printed up for me as a favor by a neighbor, in which I offered my time for basic manual labor services. That summer, I landed work helping a middle-aged man remodel his house. This involved tearing down a room, taking off and putting on a roof, and doing some basic masonry work. This consumed most of my summer and I probably earned an average of three dollars an hour. He was shrewd; I was not. This expanded into a window washing "account" for an elderly woman, periodic gutter cleaning for another elderly woman, and periodic yard work for a few other local neighborhood families. For my age, and at the time, I was making pretty decent money in my spare time (a couple of thousand dollars a year is a lot of money at that age). Not seeing a need to reinvest it at the time, most of it got spent on bike parts, a partial payment on a motorized "mini-bike," bubble gum, soda, video games, and a gold necklace and cross for my mother. It was great. I was making something of my life. I was convinced I was going to build an empire and retire by thirty. I knew there had to be more out there for me.

Having grown up in a very poor family, in a broken home, and with an alcoholic father whom I was determined to help the family get away from, entrepreneurial success wasn't just a thrill for me—it was an imperative necessity. My entrepreneurial spirit continued to play out throughout my teen years. But I knew any job I could get at that age wasn't going to solve my family's problems.

I decided I needed to go "big time." I was going to write a book. At the age of fourteen, I had been introduced to a sport called "flatlanding"—a form of freestyle bike riding on an open area of flat land. (If you aren't familiar with it, look up a flatlanding video online.) I had perfected the bar spin, the tail spin, the "endo," and a few other freestyle moves. Unfortunately, I couldn't afford a bicycle with the proper brakes on it to allow me to advance much further, but my passion for it did. At the time, there was no YouTube to look up videos on and any information I could find online that instructed you how to perform more advanced tricks was scattered and hard to find. I compiled all of the information and knowledge I needed to put together the first-ever how-to book on flatlanding. I was going to cash in. Retirement by the age of thirty seemed like a sure thing through my fourteen-year-old eyes. Then, something happened that I'll never forget. Dozens of hours into the project, the computer I was typing it on (which had been picked up out of someone's trash) crashed, and my file was lost. The feeling of panic and dread that set in as I realized all of my hard work and research was gone forever was overwhelming. I was so distraught over it that the thought of going back and recreating everything was too much to stomach. I decided to move on.

At sixteen, I started a custom engine cover production service with a friend—my first legitimate registered business—Custom Cover Productions. Using the internet, which was just starting to become a more popular household service, we were able to meet auto-enthusiasts online who had an interest in having us customize the engine covers for their Pontiacs. We sold a handful (at about $150 each) and I saw promise in the industry. While also working at a factory, I decided to become an authorized PlasmaGlow dealer, and invest some of my money ($1,700) in accessory lighting for car enthusiasts. This decision was ahead of one of the biggest auto shows on the east coast, at which we decided we would rent some vendor space and sell my merchandise. My friend paid for the vendor space, the hotel, and the car ride, while I invested in the product. We left home at 2 a.m. and got to the auto show by 8 a.m., just in time to set up for a 9 a.m. start time. I was about to earn a lot of money—or so

I thought. At the end of the two-day outdoor event, the only thing I had actually earned was a bad sunburn. I left, demoralized and with $1,700 of merchandise I had no idea what to do with. I had to make something happen to help my situation at home. I was dissatisfied and unfulfilled.

I decided I would do something related to an idea I actually had an interest in (I had absolutely no interest in cars or custom automotive lighting). I had made the mistake that so many people pursuing something greater out of life make: I had engaged in the pursuit of something just because the opportunity was there and I felt I should "do something." Many of our youth are making this same mistake right now as they prepare to bury themselves in debt to go to college to pursue something for no other reason really than because they feel like they should—or worse, because their parents feel like they should. They're about to attempt to live someone else's dream. Almost inevitably this leads to disillusionment and a sadness that can usually only be overcome by an investment of time to work on accepting the fact that much of our most precious resource—our time—was wasted going through the motions instead of planning our life based on what makes us feel fulfilled. I'm sure that many of you reading this can relate.

Since having learned how to do pushups in second grade (and going home each day to test myself on how many I could do), exercise and fitness had been a nearly constant thread throughout my life. I knew there was a warped perception by the mainstream about the bodybuilding subculture. In the pursuit of the improvement of physique, many bodybuilders were seen as boneheaded Neanderthals. I knew, as one of them, that this really was not true. I also knew that many bodybuilders resented this stereotype and would, if given the chance, make the statement that they were mainstream and intelligent. I felt this could be accomplished through contemporary fashion. I created a tagline—"This is Sport"—that I felt captured the essence of what I was trying to do with bodybuilding: help legitimize it as a mainstream sport.

Despite not having an artistic bone in my body, I decided I would draw out some graphical concepts based on some design styles I saw coming out of popular brands of clothing at the time. After drawing them out, I paid a friend to create the digital graphic designs. They looked great. I had finally found something I was passionate about, which was also a great money-making opportunity. I registered the company as High Performance Active Wear in December of 2003 and submitted the design concepts (overlaid onto digital images of the actual articles of clothing) to the CEO of Bodybuilding.com, which, at the time, was still in its infancy but already had a very large audience (they are now the largest online supplement retailer in existence, with annual revenues around half a billion dollars), and for which I was a freelance writer. After getting a favorable reply, saying they were interested in carrying my clothing—and feeling once again that I was about to make big things happen—I took my designs to a local print shop and, using the money I had earned at the factory, invested about $2,000 into having the actual clothing purchased and printed on. I sent samples over to Bodybuilding.com, which, by the way, offered very few clothing options. I was about to break through to a large distribution channel in a completely unsaturated marketplace with almost no competition. My retirement by the age of thirty was looking good again and I felt I was about to turn things around for my family.

Three weeks later, I was feeling completely different about the situation. The Bodybuilding.com team was giving me the cold shoulder. E-mail replies from my contact were taking longer and longer. He assured me he was reviewing the samples with his team but it felt like my opportunity was slipping. I learned one of my first real business lessons: a sale is not a sale until you have the money in your hand. I was banking on their interest without a firm commitment or order. Psychologically, this was very demoralizing to me and, after a few more attempts at getting other online retailers to become interested in carrying my clothing, I decided—at seventeen years old—that I was going to strike out and start my own online e-commerce store to sell my own clothing. I learned how to set one up and how to do some basic programming, built it, and got ready to rake in the cash.

It failed.

Even after that failure, the pursuit to build a large, successful business continued. I added sports supplements to the e-commerce store and tried to focus on selling them. It failed. I became a certified fitness trainer and became the first in my area to offer in-home fitness training services. It failed. I decided to add fitness consulting services to the website and use the notoriety I was gaining through my bodybuilding competitions and fitness modeling to boost website sales of supplements and clothing. It failed.

I was twenty-two years old. Not only had all of my entrepreneurial pursuits and attempts at building significant revenue for myself failed—I had failed. I had failed at creating enough revenue to be able to change the situation for my family at home. I was disillusioned, unfulfilled, and frustrated, and my sense of self-efficacy and self-worth had taken a nose dive. What was I doing with my life? Most of my friends had graduated college by that point and started their careers. I was barely finishing up community college and had, apparently—despite having been driven and consumed by faith, desire, and action for over a decade while they all enjoyed themselves—accomplished almost nothing with my life. I had wanted it so badly, to the point of tears on many occasions, and there I sat. Empty handed. Broke. Seemingly unable to change my circumstances in life. Maybe there really was something about growing up on the wrong side of the tracks that kept people down. Poverty threatened to drown me, and I didn't know how to swim.

At this point, you may be thinking to yourself, "What's to be confused about? You've found your passion. You're an entrepreneur." And, at the time, I would have agreed. I was driven and passionate about giving rise to financial success through entrepreneurialism. In fact, I had had that spirit since I was a young boy. But that entrepreneurial zeal was nothing more than a means to a bigger end, which I was infinitely more passionate about: helping my family overcome hardship.

At the age of twenty-two, my circumstances both in my household and among my family members had changed. Despite having never achieved any entrepreneurial success to really speak of, my mother and I—and a couple of my siblings—packed our stuff up and moved out while my father was at work. This closed a huge chapter in my life. Without the constant pressure and need to change my family situation, the entire focus of my life began to shift and lead me to discover my ultimate passion. I was no longer consumed with improving my situation or my family and, finally, a seed that had been planted many years ago began to grow.

When I was sixteen years old, I had traveled down from New York to North Carolina to compete in a NASA-sponsored powerlifting competition, during which I broke the national bench press record for my age group and weight class. That was my first real excursion outside of my immediate area in New York. When I arrived at the hotel in which the competition was being held, I walked through the doors and was virtually instantly changed forever. The energy inside the hotel was palpable, and there were people engaging in life everywhere I looked. People were experiencing the world. I was watching it happen, and it wasn't my own. For the first time ever, I felt a true psychological, spiritual, and personal connection to the rest of the world. I clearly saw that the rest of the world's joy, happiness, sorrow, stress, worry, surprise, confusion, and feelings of inadequacy were just as real as mine. Some might call this growing up. For most, it happens over a period of years as we grow and mature. For me, it happened very rapidly, if not all at once.

That experience stuck with me. Later that year, while traveling down to the auto show in the middle of the night to sell my Plasma-Glow lighting, I began jotting down notes. It was a list of qualities and experiences all humans share regardless of their geographic locations, cultures, genders, or points in history. Experiences that connect us. Anticipation, fear, food sharing, daily routines, etc. I later learned that there was a name for these attributes. They were called "human universals" by anthropologists. This concept of human universals united me with the rest of the world, which felt pretty profound.

What set in over the coming years was an increasingly strong connection to others who were experiencing human suffering. Naturally, I could relate most strongly to the type of struggles I had experienced myself—namely, financial struggle, or, to put it bluntly, poverty. I could understand first-hand the impediment to self-actualization that poverty carried with it.

What could I do? I was connected to the world and feeling the weight of human struggling and suffering. While I wasn't taking on the world's problems personally, the same passion and desire I had developed for helping my family began growing out to the larger world. I swore that "when I finally made it" I was going to make sure as many other people as possible made it with me. In the meantime, I would continue throwing what little "scraps" I could to non-profit organizations that were helping to alleviate world poverty and hunger.

One night, while having a conversation with Maria Blon, I heard a story that changed the way I viewed my abilities and what I would settle for. I heard the story of Jean Elie. Jean Elie was a four-year-old boy who gave to death. That's not a typo. He literally gave himself to death. As a student at the Ecole Mixte des Sibert school in Haiti—which Maria's daughter, a contributing author to this book, was an instrumental part of—Jean Elie, from a truly poor family, was guaranteed at least one meal each day. Hungry as he was, at only four years old, he decided not to eat many of those meals but to take them home to his starving family instead. As a result of his giving heart, he tragically died of malnutrition. Hearing about this sparked something in me. At that moment, just donating my scraps when I had some wasn't enough.

I didn't have a lot to give, financially, but others did. So instead of focusing on what I couldn't give or what I would give if I could, I started focusing on what others could give and how I could get them to give it. In the following days, the "I am Jean Elie" project was conceived, and my lifelong passion finally had a vehicle. The "I am Jean Elie" project's purpose is to spread Jean Elie's story, and to use his example to inspire others to share what they have with others.

With the experience in web development I had gained throughout my various entrepreneurial pursuits while growing up (remember that e-commerce store I opened up?), I had built up and was running a budding internet marketing company—my first entrepreneurial success, which, despite my many earlier "failures" (learning experiences), resulted in many accomplishments and proud moments. The success of that company also allowed me to spawn the "I am Jean Elie" project and was the catapult from which I was going to kick-start the pursuit of my real passion—finally. The first thing I did was set up a website, iamjeanelie. com (please visit), and that kicked the project off.

The fundraising got off to a great start and Jean Elie's story was inspiring everyone it was shared with. The project received coverage in the newspaper and in local business networking circles. This coverage, along with some social media promotion I developed and ran, was really gaining momentum and key objectives were planned.

First on the list: buy Jean Elie's family a new house. They desperately needed one, and it also served as a "thank you" for letting us use his story. That objective was accomplished in the latter part of 2013. The home construction was made possible after a very successful and inspiring "I am Jean Elie" kickoff event on an incredibly hot July Saturday during which we organized a day of outdoor live entertainment, including live band performances, a live DJ, food, displays of authentic Haitian hand-made artwork, silent auctions, raffles, and other enjoyable events. (You can see footage from the kickoff event at iamjeanelie.com.)

With the house complete, the "I am Jean Elie" project is now focusing on developing new ways to generate recurring revenues to support self-sustainable food programs and education using the model of "sharing"—a concept which Jean Elie embodied. I am using both my Internet marketing experience, knowledge I had gained throughout all of my previous business pursuits leading up to this point, and my formal business education—which culminated in an MBA in December 2013.

Striving for this goal of self-sustaining food programs and education is an on-going pursuit. It is the wind at my back. It is my passion. For those still striving to find their passion, I think that's exactly what passion is: a pursuit. A pursuit of something bigger and greater than yourself. If you'd like to become a part of my pursuit, please visit my project at www.iamjeanelie.com for more details.

Anthony's Lesson: Continuing to Strive and Improve to Help People

Anthony has lived through much suffering in his life, yet continues to have a strong desire to help people. The wind pushing Anthony is his deep care and love for people, which was evident in his strong desire at a young age to lift his family from poverty through his numerous entrepreneurial adventures and, now, through his passion to help people in Haiti and around the world with the "I am Jean Elie" project.

Reflection

Do the challenges in your life seem too big to even consider helping other people? You may think, "How could I even consider trying to battle a huge world problem such as hunger as Anthony has?" Take some time to examine what your biggest obstacle to happiness is right now.

Step out of your sphere of concerns to consider this: Are there people in your community or the world who are dealing with a similar issue, possibly in an even bigger way? Feel compassion for their situation and find a small act of kindness to help them. Could you expand this small act, possibly inspiring more people to join your cause and make a difference? You may find that taking a break from dwelling on your problems gives you a new perspective.

Helping people just plain feels really good. It can lift you to a new place where what you initially viewed as a huge problem seems manageable.

POSITIVE MOMENTS THAT TAKE MY BREATH AWAY

Charles Yarnold

They say that you will remember exactly where you were when something significant happens in your life. Whether that moment is good or bad, you remember exactly who you were with, the time of day, and what you were doing. One of these moments happened for me on June 18th, 2005.

Until then, I had always loved the quote "Life is not measured by the number of breaths we take, but by the moments that take our breath away." That quote implies that these moments are positive, therefore I respectfully disagree. I contend that the second half should read: ". . . but by the *positive* moments that take your breath away."

It was the summer of 2005, in between my junior and senior years of college. I was pursuing a dream of mine to become a financial planner. I had always loved working with money, investing, and finance. The opportunity and privilege of being able to help someone achieve his or her financial success felt like a perfect career path for me.

I had earned my licenses as a full-time registered agent at Northwestern Mutual, which specializes in life insurance. When you begin your career with Northwestern Mutual, they encourage you to start by scheduling meetings with your friends and family, because you are likely to be most comfortable with them when discussing products and services.

I decided to start with the most easy-going person that I have ever known. He was my role model, my idol, my best friend: my father. My father didn't have insurance and he wanted to leave a legacy to me and my brother. I figured that he would be a perfect candidate for crafting a life insurance plan. I suggested him to my mentor at Northwestern and we began planning.

While preparing for the first meeting, my mentor asked me some basic questions concerning my father's background and medical history. I told him that my father was relatively healthy for someone his age, but that he did have a tremor in his hand and jaw, which was nothing serious.

Which brings us to Saturday, June 18th, 2005. My very first appointment as a financial advisor. I cannot begin to tell you how excited, nervous, and hopeful I was to begin my career. My mentor and I were at my father's house, the place where I grew up, the place where my best memories were created. My mentor was doing the talking; I was observing and listening. He was walking us through the life insurance application. Simple, normal questions. My dad's name, date of birth, social security number. Then he began to ask the medical questions. I noticed my father's demeanor start to change. My mentor asked, "Do you have any medical conditions that I should be aware of?"

Time seemingly stood still. I will never forget the look on my dad's face. "I have Parkinson's Disease," he answered. That took my breath away. To that day he had always told me he had tremors and it was nothing serious. Finding that kind of information out is traumatic enough— imagine finding it out in front of someone I just recently met, my business mentor.

Keeping a straight face and not shedding a tear at that moment was honestly one of the most challenging things that I have ever had to go through. I wasn't sure how to react to finding out that my father has a horrific neurological disease.

My father looked at me. "You already knew that, right?" He had never told me. Maybe he just assumed I knew? Maybe he didn't know what to say? "Of course," I lied. I was wishing I could have been anywhere else at that moment.

When we were walking back out to my car, my mentor asked me, "How do you think it went?"

"Pretty good I guess," I replied. I knew he could sense something was wrong but wasn't asking. Then I told him the truth. "Actually, I didn't know he had Parkinson's."

That night, when I returned to my parents' house from the work-day, I pretended nothing had changed. I didn't want my father to feel awkward or ashamed for any reason, but tension filled the air.

I just didn't know what to say.

A few weeks went by until I built up the courage to ask him some questions. He told me that his doctors had suspected he had Parkinson's from the time he was fifty-one—seven years earlier. My father had hid-den his diagnosis for seven years. That was just the kind of man he was. He didn't want us to worry about him. Later on, he confessed that the only person he told was my aunt, his sister, who is a nurse. He didn't want anyone feeling bad or sorry for him.

He told me that he thought that a career path as a financial advisor was a great choice for me. He went on to explain to me that, when he was younger, his advisor at the time had never told him about Long Term Care, and that he wasn't able to get it now that he had Parkinson's. This potentially would be a big problem in planning his financial future. Until that moment, I had had a desire to be a financial advisor to help people and make a living, but that lit a fire in me that burns to this day. I saw firsthand, early on in my career, how powerful and important financial planning can be.

My passion for financial planning stems primarily from that mo-ment, from those conversations with my father. As a financial planner, I can help shape and build someone's future. Whether or not clients invest in what I recommend is up to them, but it is up to me to educate them on their options. I only wish that I had been able to recommend Long Term Care to my father prior to his diagnosis. One day, he may need long-term care support, which could potentially cost him hundreds of thousands of dollars.

Finding out about my father's diagnosis changed my life complete-ly. It changed how I acted, and how I *reacted*. For me, things were imme-diately put into perspective. Until then, I had always been a typical kid, getting upset when my food wasn't tasty, when someone was late, when a shoelace broke. But all of these were insignificant things in the long run. Life isn't about the small things. Life is about the relationships I build, the people I meet, and the journey along the way. Now when I see people get annoyed, angry, or upset with little nuisances, I understand, but I feel inside that it is such a waste of energy. I do not get involved or ever say anything, but I always wish I could put things in perspective for them. Life is too short to worry about things that really have no impact on my life or well-being. I realize that there is a fine line between bottling up emotions and being able to brush things off.

Since that moment with my father, I have learned to talk things through to those who bother or upset me, and brush the little things off that have no significance in my life. There is a second event in my life that has had a big impact on my perspective. It was also unexpected. Several years ago, I started participating in the local chapter of BNI, which Maria Blon also joined. After several meetings, conversations, and presentations, I still wasn't 100% sure exactly what it was that Maria did for people. I wanted to experience how she motivated, how she inspired, how she changed people's perspectives. I had a general understanding, but I wanted to learn more. Our networking group, BNI, is based on the *Givers Gain* philosophy. How would I be able to properly refer her without knowing exactly what she does?

So I signed up for Maria's eight-week class with the intention of gaining a better understanding of what she did. Never did I think for a second that the class would change my life.

I learned how to step out of my comfort zone into a place that I was not used to going. I learned that taking chances and being myself are the ways through which I want to live my life. I have always been independent and a free thinker, but I rarely took big steps and took big chances.

She also taught me more about time management, a field that I thought I was extremely good at already. In my profession, financial planning, time management is essential for running a solid practice. If I am not efficient, both I and my clients lose.

In addition, and this is perhaps the most important lesson, I have learned to value and enjoy my down time. Time spent with my family and friends is invaluable. Also, I realized that I need time away from work to enjoy life to the fullest. In 2013, nine years into my career, I took the most time off from work that I ever had—roughly three weeks. If I had to guess, I would say that I had taken three weeks *total* in the prior eight years. I have spent more time with my family, friends, and girlfriend doing the things I love and making the memories I will never forget. It is very important to be dedicated—and I love my profession—but I have learned that it is also important to live my life to the fullest.

Initially, I worried that my business would suffer as a result of less time spent focusing on the job and on my clients, but 2013 was actually my best year in business. My theory is that more time off has rejuvenated me and I actually work that much harder during the time that I do spend on business. And I have been working smarter. Less time is being wasted on non-important work. I spend more time focusing on what really matters to my clients and, therefore, my clients are happier and I am able to be in the mindset where a little time off is okay and well deserved. My clients—and I—are happier now that I have been working this new and improved schedule.

Looking back at the life lessons I have learned from my father's illness and Maria's class, I feel that I have been blessed. I have learned how fragile life is and how important it is to enjoy every minute. I have become a more grateful person, and I learned at a young age some very valuable tools that I will use not only in my life but that, hopefully, my future children will have as well.

There are so many people who walk around unhappy and unmotivated. I wish everyone could put things in perspective a little easier. Too many people focus on what they don't have instead of what they do have. Life is a blessing, and tomorrow is never promised.

Looking forward, I am extremely optimistic. I can see my relationships growing. I can envision my business going to new levels. I am looking forward to seeing new places, and traveling to places I never thought I would go.

Charles's Lesson: Taking time off benefits my life and business

Charlie learned that spending more time with his family, while taking a break from work, offered him more rewards than he ever expected. Not only did he have a wonderful time going on more vacations with his family, but he also earned more money for his business.

Reflection

How many vacation days have you taken over the last year? Are you ready to recharge, spend time with family and return with new perspectives and optimism? Vacations don't need to be long or expensive, but they do take planning. Find an activity that you are passionate about and that possibly your family or friends might also enjoy. Take out your calendar and consider starting small by scheduling a day activity at first, or even a family walk in a park. Simply planning a fun activity gets people excited and looking forward to the future.

Choosing Laughter and Healing

Rosita Labousse

Rosita is the sweetest, most positive and cheerful woman whom I have ever met. She lives across the street from the school in Merger, Croix-des-Bouquet, Haiti, is in charge of the cafeteria kitchen, and has cooked many delicious meals for us. I am grateful that Shad translated for me when I interviewed Rosita for this story.

Rosita lives in a three-room house with concrete walls and floors and sparse furnishings. She cooks on a wood fire outside, and has no well and no bathroom. She has six children living in her house—some are hers, some she has unofficially adopted—and many visitors, especially from the orphanage where she worked as a custodian for many years. There are pigs and chickens, dogs and kittens, all grateful for Rosita's loving embrace and care. Every time I see her, she is smiling which makes everyone around her feel happier. Rosita had been saving for one and a half years to save up enough money to build an outhouse, which was under construction during my last visit. Until it is built, the family will continue to go to the bathroom in the woods. When I was there, the septic had been dug. In the hot sun and with smiles on their faces, Rosita's older children were mixing and carrying concrete to the mason, which he spread on the cinder block walls.

I feel lucky to have received Rosita's love and healing. When I arrived in Haiti on December 31, 2013, I had a relentless cough and sore throat. Through broken Creole and waving hands, I conveyed my problem to Rosita. She went out to her garden to pick herbs and flowers, started a fire in the sweltering heat so that she could boil water, and made me a healing salt tea that helped my throat tremendously. Rosita sent a carafe of tea, carefully wrapped in a clean linen with me. The next morning, her son Wolson arrived on his bicycle with a fresh batch of tea for me. What a lovely surprise to start my day!

Later that day, Rosita arrived with her children with all of the fixings for pumpkin soup, the traditional meal in Haiti on New Year's Day. In the early days of slavery on the island, only land owners and people of wealth were given pumpkin soup. So, after earning their independence from France, the Haitian people started the tradition of eating pumpkin soup to celebrate on New Year's Day. Rosita and a few teens stayed up all night to make us delicious Pumpkin Soup to celebrate the New Year. They were laughing and joking the whole time they cooked over the smoky charcoal. She had the biggest smile on her face in the morning and was such a pleasure to be around, despite having no sleep at all.

Rosita would like her children to be able to attend university so that they can be successful. She saves as much money as possible from these jobs: selling charcoal, raising pigs, and working at the school. Donna King, who is on the HEART board, is helping Rosita and her family in the mountains to get a coffee business started. Unfortunately, Rosita's husband drains the family's resources rather than contributing. He keeps roosters for cock fighting, rather than raising chickens for food. Rosita told us that the most challenging time of her life was when her oldest daughter, Woslina, was born. She had been living at her husband's cousin's house and was kicked out on a rainy night with a three-day-old baby to sleep outside. I couldn't fathom how Rosita had the strength not only to get up each day, but to do so with such joy. Rosita says, "Children keep me going. I love having them around me. We are always joking and having fun."

When somebody in her family gets sick, Rosita knows the herbs that will help them get better, and she knows that there are different herbs that work for children and adults. This healing tradition was passed down to her from her mother when she grew up in the country. Rosita keeps all of this knowledge in her head, using it to help the lucky people in her community family.

Rosita and Carina are very close. When Rosita found out that Carina was moving back to the US, she was heartbroken. While Rosita cared for Carina in many ways—from cooking for her and doing her wash, to listening, laughing with and telling inspirational stories—Rosita was also grateful to Carina because she always noticed when the family did not have food and would give some to her. Carina also noticed when Rosita's son Wolson was sick, and arranged to have him taken to the hospital, saving his life.

The best way that I can describe Rosita is that she is a joyful saint to children, adults, plants, and animals. I feel lucky whenever I spend time in her beautiful company.

This poem came to me on Mother's Day when I was meditating:

> *Her husband's interests are his*
> *Cock(s)*
> *Fighting*
> *Women*
> *Send your wife out in the rain with a three-day-old baby.*
>
> *Yet, when I see her beautiful smile,*
> *I feel love.*
> *Watch the children and animals gather round your beauty and grace,*
> *knowing they have a home with you,*
> *Rosita*

Rosita's Lesson: Choosing to Laugh

We always have a choice about how to react to any given situation. Rosita's story shows us how it is possible to find the best in any given situation. She laughs to ease not only her tension but that of everyone around her.

Reflection

Can you relate to the many hardships Rosita has endured, some written here and some you might imagine? How might Rosita's story inspire you to look beyond your challenges to find what you do have control over?

You can always choose your attitude in any given situation. For example, there are times in my life when someone might speak to me in a hurtful way. I know that, if I don't address the issue and process the hurt that I feel in a healthy way, then without realizing what I am doing, I will speak with anger and impatience to someone whom I love who has nothing to do with the other situation. Sometimes I need to blow off steam by using humor to diffuse strong emotions. If I can laugh at a situation, I heal myself, creating a healthier attitude from which everyone around me benefits.

Think of a situation in your life where you could use humor and a smile to transform a challenge into a situation that helps you. Notice the effect that positive reaction has on you and the people around you.

My Journey from Homeless to Building a Family, Home, and Career

Vilma Fyke

My mother and four brothers lived in an apartment in Brooklyn after my parents split when I was two years old. My dad would visit us after school so he felt involved with us, but I imagine it wasn't easy for my mom to raise four kids mostly on her own. When I was four years old and my grandmother visited, she kept saying that I wasn't helping enough.

My mom was often sick and would go in and out of the hospital. I didn't know what was wrong with her, as nothing was ever talked about. We weren't allowed to ask questions. (I found out, when I was an adult, that she had cancer.) My mom often said that she was sick because of me. I don't know why she blamed me, but I heard it a lot. One morning, when I was ten, I went to wake her up. She was breathing, but I couldn't wake her up. My dad called an ambulance and took her to the hospital. I kept asking if I could bring her pajamas to her, and would hear no response from him. I found out—three days later—that she had died. I felt horrible and, as you can imagine, I had a lot of guilt for a girl of just ten years old. I have compassion for my mom now because she was sick and didn't know how to process all that was happening to her and care for me.

Life changed when my dad and my stepmother came to live with me and my brothers. I didn't ever feel at home after that. There were just too many things that made me feel like a guest in their house. My stepmother brought her son with her. He had the run of the house and we had to cater to him. For instance, if I was watching TV and he came into the room, I had to change the channel to the station he wanted to watch. So I left home at fifteen, trying to find a place that felt like home again.

I was pretty much homeless for four years. I always managed to find a place to sleep, mostly at friends' houses, climbing in their bedroom windows when their parents went to sleep. One of my friends used to want to escape to be with her boyfriend. We both had long brown hair, so I would get in her bed and pretend to be her, and she would go off to be with him.

If I couldn't find a friend to stay with, I slept in cars or camped out, but those times were rare. On the mornings after I had slept in cars, one of my friends would have me crawl into her bedroom window. I would sneak into the bathroom, take a shower, get dressed, crawl out of the window, and head to school. I don't think that anyone knew that I was homeless because I kept taking turns at different friends' houses. I made a lot of friends, and I rarely felt scared, but it was a lonely life. I didn't meet any other people on the street. I always managed to get washed up and ready for school. No teachers knew. My two best friends at the time moved away so nobody knew. I hung out with hippies and partiers. Nobody asked questions. There was a brief period where I lived with a guy, but he was abusive. He hit me and I decided to live on the streets rather than live with a guy who hits me. I had more self-worth than that.

Finding food could be a problem, though. I remember, one day, I had forty-five cents, which was enough to buy a piece of pizza. When I walked into the pizza place, my friend asked me if I wanted the other half of his sandwich. I said "Sure," sat down with him, took a bite, and looked up wide-eyed at him saying, "Is this meat?" He laughed and said, "No it is eggplant." I hadn't eaten anything substantial in so long, that that half sandwich felt like a feast.

I was always a people watcher and often sat back and observed how people behaved. Most adults were not helpful and some were really horrible to me. I wasn't someone who most adults would care for. I think this was due to my distrust of adults. The adults that I knew seemed unconscious, irrational, and not to be trusted. In school, we were asked to raise our hands to ask questions and then, when we did, the teachers would yell at us. My stepmom would make me hang up the phone if someone called me. There was no discussion, and I wasn't allowed to discuss or ask questions. When I left home, I didn't want any adults to find out that I was homeless because I was worried that they might send me home or to a foster home.

I had always looked at life as an adventure with endless possibilities. Even when I was homeless, I was sure I was right. I met many amazing people and had fun. In the middle of my senior year, a woman picked me up when I was hitchhiking and asked where I lived. I sensed that I could trust her, so I told her I was homeless. She told me she would give me money for an apartment, and that I could work it off cleaning her house. I was in heaven. I loved that apartment. I was right to trust her as she was an interesting, amazing, empowering woman in her late fifties or sixties, who was writing her own book. It was so sweet of her to pick me up and help me out.

I was in that apartment for about six or seven months before I ended up leaving because an old boyfriend was stalking me. He had broken into my apartment and held a rifle to my head, saying that if I didn't take him back he'd kill both of us. It was a scary situation. I didn't take him back, but was able to satisfy him by lifting the restraining order that I had previously filed against him at the police station. So, once again, I was homeless because I didn't want him to find me.

I still kept going to school, because I enjoyed learning. I really wanted to graduate. The teachers, at that time, made it extremely difficult for me and were actually abusive. I didn't fit the norm and they had no tolerance for that. I loved to read, but, in my senior year, I forgot to bring a book to my favorite class—contemporary literature. The teacher berated me for what seemed like an eternity. At some point, I rolled my eyes. He walked over to my desk and slapped me so hard I fell out of my chair onto the floor. I was so shocked and scared that I just ran out of the class. A guy in the class walked up to the teacher after I ran out and punched him. While this young man could clearly feel that I had been treated unjustly, his method of trying to help made problems worse for both of us. He was expelled and not allowed to graduate. I was suspended from school because the teacher lied and said that I had been disruptive.

On the day that I went to pick up my cap and gown, excited that

I was getting closer to my goal of graduating, the school informed me that I would not graduate due to not passing that English class. I went on a drinking binge after that, because it was a way to "not feel." I didn't have anyone to defend me in a productive way, and ended up having to go summer school to get my diploma. They didn't have the contemporary literature class that I wanted to take in summer school, so I ended up taking remedial English. I was absolutely devastated. I went to summer school completely drunk every day and still got a 99%. Despite what seemed like a conspiracy to keep me from graduating, I earned my diploma. It didn't feel like an accomplishment, though, because there was no cap and gown ceremony. When my parents didn't come, it made me even more sad.

After finally graduating, I decided to join the navy so I could become a doctor. I had taken nursing in high school, but had decided it wasn't the way I wanted to help people. Something about it seemed limiting. I thought that, in the navy, I could get a free education, travel, and always have a place to sleep. Life had different plans for me, though.

Just before I went into the navy, I had re-started seeing a guy I was truly in love with. I had originally met him when I was fifteen, pointed at him, and said, "That will be my husband someday." I always felt like he was the one for me, though I am not sure why. We would date, then break up, over and over. Even though we were intensely attracted to each other, he wouldn't commit to a relationship. The summer that I graduated, we started seeing each other again. Our relationship wasn't moving forward, and, as much as I loved him, I decided to move ahead without him. I didn't even tell him that I had joined the navy to better myself through education. While friends were having a going away party for me at our favorite bar, he walked in and asked me why I was at this party. He was shocked that I was leaving the next day and was going to be sent to Florida.

I reported to the navy office the next morning. They did a pregnancy test, which showed negative, so off I went to basic training. I actually enjoyed basic training. I loved being physical, and thought that the techniques they used to break people down were kind of ridiculous. I couldn't understand why anyone took it personally when they were yell-ing at us, calling us names. After all, they didn't know me or my mother, both of whom they said horrible things about. (My mom had been dead for nine years. I highly doubt she was sleeping around.) The inculcation in the navy was intended to break people down so that they wouldn't feel bad and get upset in future challenging circumstances. I couldn't understand why other girls would cry when they were getting yelled at or had to run an extra lap.

One day during training, I had jumped off the high dive and lost my breath. The officer was screaming at me, telling me not to hold on to the side of the pool. I pushed her because I was panicking and couldn't breathe. I was sent off for "punishment." But it didn't feel like punishment to me. We just had to exercise more, which brought the other girls to tears. The officers saw how tough I was, though, and put me in a specialized company that I loved because it offered more challenge. I always simply found a way around things, instead of getting upset. I would laugh in my head at what was happening around me.

As I was about to finish my basic training and be shipped off to tech school, I was called in to the doctor's office because something had shown up on my blood work that week. I was nervous, wondering if I had something serious. When the doctor told me I was pregnant, I said that it was impossible since I hadn't been with anyone the whole time I was in basic training—and they had done a pregnancy test the day I started. He said the first test was a urine test, which was not as accurate as blood work. I was one week away from graduating. You can imagine how devastating it was. Once again I didn't get to graduate. I was immediately put in another unit, waiting to be shipped out.

Ironically, I was put into the unit that I had once been told had "crazy people" in it who couldn't handle basic training. Nobody from the other units would make eye contact with the people in that unit, thinking they were all crazy people. Those "crazy people" turned out to be people just like me, all getting shipped out for various reasons. Nevertheless, since I had nothing to lose and I wouldn't see those people again, I acted "crazy" to amuse myself. When we walked to lunch, people would look at us weirdly. I would twitch and make funny noises, watching the faces of the other people. I laughed about it and had fun.

Thankfully, I received an honorable discharge. Even so, the commanding officer who drove three of us off base said that we disgusted him. The feeling was mutual. I was pregnant. I wasn't crazy.

I decided to stay in Florida and have the baby. I called a friend's mother, whom I had been close to, and asked if I could stay with her until I had the baby. She said yes, but asked me to first go to New York and tell my boyfriend that he was going to be a father. I didn't want to, but got on the plane. The last I had heard was that my old boyfriend was in Alaska looking for land to homestead. When I got to New York, I went to a bar that we used to hang out at, hoping one of his friends could give me an address where I might reach him. Lo and behold, he walked in shortly after I did. We had both gotten in that day—me from Florida, he from Alaska. He said that, on the way to Alaska, he had told his friend that he should have asked me to marry him instead of letting me go into the navy. He got down on one knee right there in the bar and asked me to marry him, and I told him he was going to be a father. We married a month later. We've been married thirty-two years, now, and have two children.

I had never wanted kids, but I was a kid of nineteen when I gave birth to my son. When the nurse put him in my arms, I felt like I came alive. I had loved being pregnant, and I absolutely loved being a mom and understood what love was. It was like I had been blind and was now seeing color for the first time. I healed with my children. Because of all I had been through, I had learned how not to treat children. I was a stay at home mom and gave my kids a lot of attention, but not in a spoiled way.

My son could read by the time he was two. I would read to him, we would listen to music, we played games, and I rocked them a lot. I was strict when it came to discipline. They had their bed and bath times, and at the end of the day playing with them, it was time for bed at 7 pm. Then it was time for my husband. I wanted them to see that we were a united couple. I think that made them feel secure. I didn't even have a car. I was simply home with them. I didn't feel like I needed to escape; I was just with my kids. I was fortunate, because my dad and stepmom came back into my life and loved my children. We found that we had amazing grandparents on both sides, so that my husband and I could go out on a date when we wanted to. Even though my parents were only alive a couple of years after my children were born, that was a nice and healing time for me.

My children went to school for the first couple of years of elementary school. During that time, I saw how they were being treated and saw that their love of learning was being squashed at the public school. I wanted them to love learning like I loved learning, so I decided to homeschool them. I used homeschooling programs that were beautiful and rich, including novels, poetry, and much more. At one point when they were being homeschooled, they had to go in for testing. The teacher testing them didn't expect them to do well, but they earned some of the highest scores in the school district. And, eventually, they had no problem transitioning to college.

Colleges weren't sure that they could accept my son, however. They wanted him to take biology before being let in, but his scores were so high, he was accepted right away. My daughter and I both have something called Irlen Syndrome, with means that we process learning a little bit differently than most people. We can be a little dyslexic or "ADD." I have to read something three or four times to understand what I have read. Hands on, however, we learn right away. My son is now an occupational therapist who works with children who have autism, ADD, and other disorders. Recently, he decided to go back to college to earn his PhD in neuropsychology, while my daughter is a physical therapist.

When my children were still little, my father said that he wanted to share some things about himself and his family. I didn't know how my dad and mom met, and had no pictures. I didn't know anything about my grandparents. So I was so excited to learn more about the past. Less than a week later, he was having chest pains and wouldn't go to the doctor. I put him in the car, drove to the hospital, and was helping him to get out of the car when he died in my arms. I didn't realize how much of an impact my father passing away would have, because I'd lived much of my life without his support. I felt I had no closure at the time. Several years later, my stepmom and grandmother passed away. My niece, whom I had planned on raising and adopting—and who was living with us at that time—was taken back by her parents. All of those things happened in a six-month period, and, as a result, I basically had a breakdown. It took several years before I was diagnosed with lupus when I was twenty-nine years old. I had extreme fatigue, rashes, joint pain, and sores in my mouth. I would get up, take a shower, and want to go lie down again. The doctors were condescending and uncaring, and would tell me it was stress or just "in my head." I decided there had to be a better way to get healthier.

It took years to find some real help. I was skeptical when I was visiting in Tennessee and a friend took me to see someone who did alternative medicine. The practitioner muscle tested me using Kinesiology and contact reflex analysis when I was down there. Afterwards, she worked with me over the phone, suggesting changes to my diet and herbal supplements. I decided to do as she recommended, and was better in a year, plus was in remission from lupus for 10 years. (My kids didn't even know that I had lupus until a couple of years ago.)

My daughter had tinnitus, which was an irritating ringing in her ears. Doctors couldn't do anything to help her. I took my daughter to an IMB (isometric muscle balancing) practitioner who helped her on the first visit. I was skeptical, and told my daughter in front of the practitioner that if she wasn't better to be honest. My daughter said, "Mom, I really do feel better. The ringing has stopped." The combination of my and my daughter's healing was evidence enough to make me want to learn more.

I wanted to learn techniques to keep myself and my family healthy. I started taking as many seminars on energy healing as I could. I began by learning isometric muscle balancing, which had helped my daughter. I signed up for a doctor of naturopathy program, but only made it as far as my bachelor's degree, because the school closed down. I got my bachelor's degree in natural health certificate in the mail. I am now certified in IMB, Contact Reflex Analysis, Total Body Modification, Massage, Acupressure, Health Kinesiology, and Emotional Diffusion. Currently, I am learning the Emotion and Body Code. I use a biofeedback machine, ionic foot bath detox, flower essences, essential oils, and crystals on clients.

I love learning and will learn anything to help people. When I started this journey, I had no intention of making naturopathy my career.

However, I needed to practice on people to get certified. So I helped people, who told more people, and—before I knew it—my dining room had become a waiting room and I was working in my living room. When my husband saw what was happening, he said, "I need to build you an office."

I've been helping people to heal for about fifteen years. I can't imagine doing anything else I would love better. I feel so blessed that life took me in a different direction than to be a traditional nurse or doctor. From my experience, the medical profession simply gives quick fixes to help people feel better but doesn't treat the whole person, and doesn't get to the root of the problem. In contrast, with energy work I am helping people physically, emotionally, and spiritually. I don't feel that I heal people but, instead, empower them to heal themselves.

It's incredibly satisfying to see someone realize how their emotional state is connected to their physical state—and then realize they can change it. And then to see the changes in them, their relationships, and their lives is truly amazing. When people tell me about their aches and pains, I help them put an emotional story together. Sometimes, at first, they won't see connections. Then when the light bulb goes off and they make the connection, it is incredible. Watching them heal themselves is empowering—both for them and for me.

Here are a few examples of healing stories:

- When one of my clients who has lupus first started working with me, I had to go out to her car to help her walk into the house so that she could come in and sit down. Now she walks in on her own, is working and active, and is down to taking only one medicine instead of six. She doesn't need erythropoietin shots to bring her blood count up like she used to.
- One of my clients was a young child who had night terrors and I was able to help her heal. When she was sixteen, she took several classes from me: Emotional Diffusion, Muscle Testing, Herbs, Flower Essences, and Essential oils. She is intuitive and has an amazing gift for healing. At seventeen, she opened her own business in Newburgh. She has an oxygen machine and ionic foot bath at her office. She is amazing.

- One of my students learned to muscle test from her sister. She has an incredible, intuitive knack. She can pick up energy on people over long distances. She will call me up and ask me what is going on when she senses that something is off with me. I encouraged her to take the Body Code and Emotion Code certification. She is an incredible healer, which is encouraging for me.

I feel honored to help people heal and to be able to train people to heal others. I am truly grateful for all that I have gone through in my life and for all that I have now. I have always liked learning about the human body and used to look through dictionaries and encyclopedias to learn more, and now I am able to put that knowledge to work for others. When I help people, I feel like I am also healed—and I learn so much from my clients that it feels like a mutual exchange of learning and love.

Recently, I noticed myself grinding my teeth at night. During a meditation, I realized that I was nervous about exposing myself and telling my stories through this book. But it is my hope that sharing my story will help people to find their place in the world and a home where they feel safe. Being homeless for so long, I didn't always have something to eat or a bed to sleep in at night. Now that I have those things, I am so grateful for my home, food, and especially my bed. In fact, when I get into bed at night, I giggle because it feels so good. My husband is amazed that even after thirty years, I am so grateful, still giggling like a little girl.

Vilma's Lesson: Choosing a Unique Path

Vilma's story is amazing to me. I can't imagine having the courage to leave home at fifteen and view homelessness as "an adventure." I would have been much too scared, but she had such courage. She even laughed inside when being challenged in the military.

I admire how Vilma follows what feels right to her and does not compromise her values for any reason. For example, she homeschooled her children because she wanted them to love learning. Vilma's zest for learning is evident in all of the healing techniques she has studied and now uses to help people heal.

Reflection

You can view hard times with a sense of dread and loathing, but all that will do is bring your energy down and make everything worse. Vilma viewed her choice to be homeless as an adventure, which gave her the positive attitude and strength to deal with problems that came her way.

What challenge in your life could you view with a sense of adventure? Is there something that you could study in order to overcome this challenge?

Discover Love, Abundance and Joy through *The Emotion Code*

Dr. Bradley Nelson

When I look back on my life, it seems to me that all the experiences I have had have combined together to enable me to bring the message of *The Emotion Code* to the world.

When I was thirteen years old, I was diagnosed with kidney disease. At the hospital, the doctors told my parents and me that there was no treatment for what I had. They told me to be careful, and not to run or play too hard, because it could be dangerous. I remember thinking that they didn't really need to tell me that, because just walking would sometimes create pain in my back that would make me feel like I had been stabbed with a knife.

Since the disease was potentially fatal, and since there was no medical treatment for it, my parents decided to try an alternative. They took me to see a couple of alternative doctors who practiced and lived in a trailer house situated in the middle of a field on the outskirts of town. Within a couple of weeks after starting their treatments, I felt much better. The pain that I had been experiencing was much less frequent, and much less severe.

After about a month, I had just about forgotten that I was ever sick. My parents took me back to the clinic, where they ran the tests on me again. The tests were all negative, and, as I recall, that was the first time I ever heard the phrase "spontaneous remission." I knew in my heart that what my "alternative doctors" had done had worked, and I decided to become a doctor when I grew up. Not a mainstream medical doctor, but an "alternative" doctor like the doctors who had healed me. If I had to practice in a trailer house in the middle of a muddy field on the edge of town, that was okay with me. But, as the years went on, my dream of being a healer started to fade a bit. I was introduced to computer programming in college and I loved it. I loved business, and decided that I wouldn't go into the healing arts after all. Instead, I was going to become a businessman.

When I was about six months away from starting the MBA program at Brigham Young University, my wife Jean and I went home to Montana for Christmas. As we were sitting with my mother and father in their living room, my father suddenly asked me, "Are you sure you don't want to go to chiropractic school? You've always wanted to do that, and it seems like a really great career." I replied that, "No, I've decided to get my MBA." He said, "Well, why don't you think about it one more time?" I thought about it for a moment, and told him that I would consider it.

Later that evening, Jean and I drew up a list of pros and cons. On one side was chiropractic, and on the other side was the MBA and the business world. The pro list was a little longer on the chiropractic side, but I still wasn't convinced. Honestly, I was not absolutely sure what I wanted to do. I had thought that my mind was made up, but when I considered my lists I felt like I was being torn between two exciting futures.

When Jean and I got married, we had made an agreement that we would never make any momentous decision without praying about it to see if it was right. This was definitely one of those momentous decisions. So, that night found me on my knees. I essentially said, "Father in Heaven, if it makes any difference to you, please help me to know what direction to go. I will go either way." I was awakened in the middle of the night with my mind full of thoughts about healing, and how wonderful it is to be able to serve other people in a natural way. I remember thinking, "Well yes, that's true, but this other direction is good, too . . . ."

It was a long night that night. I woke up three times, and each time my mind was full of warm feelings about going into the healing arts. Somehow, I still wasn't sure. The next night found me on my knees once again, asking God for guidance. And that was a night that I will never forget if I live to be one million years old. That night, like the night before, I was awakened three times. And each time I was awakened, my mind was filled with the same thoughts as the night before. But somehow these feelings became progressively stronger and more powerful each time I was awakened. The third time that I woke up my mind was overflowing with thoughts of service to mankind and humanity.

It's impossible for me to describe what the experience was really like, but those feelings were absolutely overwhelming. As I was feeling and thinking those thoughts about service through healing and helping the world and all of humanity, a voice suddenly spoke to me. It was a voice as clear as crystal, and as distinct and as audible as anything I'd ever heard. It said, "This is a sacred calling." I had my answer, and I have never regretted my decision to heed that call.

I've reflected on this experience many times since then. I believe that because the human body is actually a "sacred temple" for our spirit to inhabit, that any time we are working to help that body function better, we are doing a sacred thing. If we are sewing up an injury, if we are helping someone who is disabled, or if we are healing someone who is in need of healing, we are doing sacred work.

I practiced as a holistic chiropractic physician for seventeen years. I made a habit, during those years, of making a silent prayer for help from God for each person whom I worked on. And, during those years, I learned bit by bit, patient by patient, case by case about the true underlying causes of our illnesses.

During the last ten years that I was in practice I was working primarily with people who had would been told there was no cure for them. These were people who would have been given up on by the Western medical establishment—people who were suffering from things like fibromyalgia, chronic fatigue syndrome, autoimmune diseases, and even cancer. There were times during those years when, in response to my silent prayer for help, information would flood into my mind about exactly what a person needed and what approach I should take. Sometimes this was a completely different way of looking at things than what I had ever imagined before. It was during those years that I gained the understanding of how our emotional baggage is a real thing that affects all of us in many dramatic ways.

During those years, I developed a very powerful feeling that people could do a lot to help themselves. I had a deep, driving urge to empower people. I began teaching seminars to do just that in 1998, and taught as many seminars to as many people as I could around the US and Canada for many years. But I was wearing myself out. I was working in my practice sixty hours a week and then flying off on weekends teaching seminars, and my family was suffering because of it. In 2002, I got a message from "upstairs" that I needed to turn my practice over to someone else, and sell everything I owned. It had become clear to me that the healing methods that I had developed were not just for me and my patients and the handful of seminar attendees that came to hear me speak. They were for the whole world—including you.

I had to get out of practice so that I would have time to write a book about what I knew. I left practice in 2004, and in June of 2007 I published *The Emotion Code: How to Release Your Trapped Emotions for Abundant Health, Love and Happiness*. The success of *The Emotion Code* has been astonishing to me. It taught me how powerful the written word is. There are people on every continent and in nearly every country on earth who are using *The Emotion Code* to get rid of their own emotional baggage, and the best part is that they are helping their loved ones to do the same. I get e-mails from people, all the time, whose lives are changing, who are falling in love as they get rid of their "Heart-Walls," or who are getting rid of their anxiety, their debilitating panic attacks, phobias, depression, their annoying discomfort, and their miserable pain. These people are so happy to feel good feelings again, instead of dark ones, and they are regaining their health again, too.

I've been all over the world teaching The Emotion Code Seminar, from Australia to Germany, from Toronto to Auckland, from Seattle to New York City, from Dublin to Amsterdam, and it's really been a wonderful adventure. While I would love to take the credit for this amazing information, I will never do that. I believe that I could not have done this without help from above. My calling is to bring *The Emotion Code* to the world and to give back the healing birthright that belongs to every man, woman, and child on this planet.

Of all the important things I have learned about human beings, the most important has to do with the heart. Ancient peoples believed that the heart was the seat of the soul, the source of our creativity, the center of love and romance, and the core of our being. Western medicine has never given any credence to these ideas, believing instead that the heart is merely a mechanical pump. However, in the 1970s, it was discovered that the heart is actually full of gray matter and white matter—the same substances that make up the brain. This discovery helped lead to the creation of a new branch of medicine called neurocardiology.

When heart transplants started to become a routine procedure back in the 1960s, it wasn't long before transplant patients began reporting strange post-surgical symptoms. These included complete changes in handwriting, as well as preferences in music, food, and sports. In fact, it was not unusual for patients to report that they suddenly had memories of cities or towns that they had never visited yet, somehow, they "knew" that they had been there before. In every case, they had somehow become possessors of the affinities and the loves and the memories of the donors. The heart is a second "brain," a brain that stores our fondest memories, our best creative ideas, and our love. It is our heart that connects us with those that we love and to our higher power.

Something that I was shown and that I have come to understand is that when we are hurt emotionally, our subconscious mind can create what I call a "Heart-Wall." Your subconscious mind will try to protect your heart with this wall, or protective shield, because your heart is the part of you that holds your most precious feelings and memories and capacities to live a beautiful life. When you read or hear about one person brutalizing another person, or abusing or hurting another person in some way, I believe that the perpetrator—if examined—would always be found to have a Heart-Wall. They were hurt by someone else and now can't feel the full extent of what they are doing to hurt others. The energies that they have collected over their lifetime of hurt are now insulating them from feeling the injury that they deal to others. The walls that we put up around our hearts, though intended to protect us from further heartache and hurt, end up disconnecting us from each other. They make us numb to life and to love.

When we are experiencing deep grief, hurt, or loss, it can actually be an assault on the deepest part of our beings. Can you recall a time in your own life when you felt like your heart was going to break? Most people can.

Is a wall around your heart contributing to physical illness or disease for you? Is your Heart-Wall hampering your ability to give and receive love? Is it interfering with your ability to feel good emotions, or contributing to your feelings of isolation? Is it creating depression, anxiety or self-sabotage for you? Is your Heart-Wall interfering with your ability to succeed?

If you are at all frustrated with your love life, your social life, your health issues, or the level of financial abundance that you've been able to attain, a Heart-Wall may be a big piece of the puzzle for you. In my experience, approximately 93% of people suffer from this phenomenon. And, when their Heart-Walls are removed, profound changes often occur for the better. I have seen the changes that take place on an individual level when a person's Heart-Wall is removed. I have seen people find love after decades of loneliness. I've seen people find success after a lifetime of disappointment. And I have had people tell me that for the first time in their lives they can "feel" the love of God for them, after their Heart-Walls were removed.

What is the global result when the vast majority of people suffer from these invisible walls around their hearts? War, genocide, racial strife, and murder. You see, we "feel" with the brain in our hearts. When that heart-brain is walled off, we are left with the dilemma of trying to "feel" with the brain in our heads, which "feels" nothing. The brain in our heads is purely logical, and thinks that it's perfectly acceptable to use war to settle differences between nations and drop bombs on defenseless civilians. The brain in our heads readily subscribes to the belief that any human suffering is justifiable if the ends are important enough to us.

If you have a Heart-Wall, can you see how important it is for you to clear it away? Can you see the importance of helping your own children and your own family? It is my hope that you will stop looking outward for the solutions to your problems, and practice some true inner healing by getting rid of the wall around your own heart. I believe that the most important thing you can do to improve your health, your love life, and your longevity is to remove your trapped emotions—and especially your Heart-Wall.

I know that this world is going to change. I know the day is coming when there will no longer be war on the face of the earth. I know the day is coming when the lamb will lie down with the lion, and there will finally be peace. I believe that the power is now within us to help bring about this new world. Start with yourself. Remove your own trapped emotions to finally let go of your own emotional baggage. Remove your own Heart-Wall. But don't stop there. Keep going. Remove the Heart-Walls from your loved ones, and from as many people as you can.

It may seem like a small thing, but the only way we can change this world is by changing it one heart at a time. We now have a way to do just that, so let's get busy. If this story resonates with your heart, if you can feel the truth of it, then I hope you will learn about this work for yourself. There is so much you can do to help yourself to get well and stay well. And there are people all around you who need help—some whom you know and love. You can help them. You can heal their lives. It's really more a matter of "remembering" than learning. Somewhere, deep inside of you, there is a mighty healer.

I am so honored to share this knowledge with you. Take a moment and visit www.EmotionCode.tv to view a series of free training videos which will walk you through the process of releasing your first trapped emotion. May God bless you to find a life as full of love, joy, and abundance as possible.

Dr. Bradley Nelson's Lesson: Listening, then Taking Action

I feel honored that Dr. Bradley Nelson has shared his beautiful healing story to inspire and heal us all. His model of listening to his intuition to heal himself and develop the Emotion Code, which is healing people around the world, is truly inspirational. Dr. Nelson's extensive collection of healing stories that validate the power of his simple technique—which can be used on people and animals in person or over long distances—is a gift to us all. How generous that he offers this extensive education to people around the world.

Intuition comes to me often with an idea popping into my head.

The idea to have Dr. Bradley Nelson write a chapter for this book popped into my head, I listened to this idea and decided to take action. I wrote an email to Dr. Nelson, asking if he would write a chapter for our book. Truthfully, I never expected to hear back from him. I was shocked when Dr. Nelson actually said yes—and that he would publicize the book, as well. I felt a bit overwhelmed by his generosity and quite frankly shocked at my own brassiness. Part of me just didn't believe that this was real. When I received Dr. Nelson's chapter, I became a believer!

Dr. Nelson is obviously a person who has found his passion, lives his passion, and shares his passion to heal people around the world. Viewing his life and career from my perspective, it seems like he has "made it" in life. Knowing that we are all a work in progress, I wonder what new adventures are in store for Dr. Nelson. His story of praying, taking time to reflect, consulting with his wife, and listening to messages from God, which guided him to follow this sacred calling, is a beautiful example that we can all learn from.

Reflection

Do you feel like you are following a sacred calling in your life, or do you feel uncertain about what your calling is? Spiritual guidance is available for each person and will come in different ways. As Ann Bell and I say in the agreements for our Online Inspiration Class, "Awakening is most often as subtle as a whisper but can be as explosive as a lightning bolt." While Dr. Nelson's awakening was more explosive, guidance more often comes in subtle ways, through noticing what feels right and wrong to you. Taking time to slow down, reflect, or pray in a way that feels right to you is a great place to start. As you have read from Dr. Nelson and my experience, listening, then taking action, can create miracles.

DANCING MY WAY TO
A BETTER LIFE

Wildo Bruny

Wildo Bruny has given me joy on each of the eight trips that I have taken to Haiti since July 2010. As Shad says, Wildo is the life of every party and everyone is always charmed by his smiles, dancing, joking, and playfulness. I love watching Wildo dance. He is great with Michael Jackson music, especially. He and his friends entertain us with their graceful, coordinated routines.

A big party was planned for Wildo's thirteenth birthday, with food and dancing, and lots of friends coming over. Wildo had been very sick with malaria for days, and we were all wondering if his party should be delayed, but Wildo kept saying that he still wanted to have it. He slept, off and on, for most of the day, not looking well. Even at the beginning of his party, he didn't look like he felt well at all. But Wildo was a gracious host and began to feel better as people arrived. As the party moved along, he seemed to glow brighter and brighter. I believe that his friends and his good attitude did as much to heal him as the medicine we got him that day.

I wanted to hear more of Wildo's story, so Shad helped me interview him by translating my English and Wildo's Creole.

Wildo was born in the mountains and was initially raised by his mother, who had a small street restaurant where she sold food. Wildo was very content and happy, attending private school with his sister. After Wildo's mother died, when he was eight, Wildo and his sister were sent down to Sibert, Croix Des Bouquets. His dad had been working at a brewery, but he had lost his job. He didn't have any money to send Wildo to school. His dad did some research and found a school that was free of charge. The problem was that Wildo had to start school from kindergarten, even though he had already been in school, which was frustrating to Wildo.

The other students would tease him because he had gone to a private school. Wildo was bored, but was always first in his class, since he had already learned the material in his other school. Wildo's dad told him to not pay attention to the kids who were teasing him, which is easier said than done, and there were times when Wildo wouldn't go to class. Now, at fifteen years old, Wildo is in fifth grade, instead of tenth grade, which is still very frustrating to him. He is going to challenge the sixth grade graduation test this year so that he can move directly to 7th grade. In order to succeed, he is tutored every day by Shad's cousin, Son, and goes to his school on Saturdays for extra preparation.

While school has been challenging for Wildo, those problems have been nothing compared to life after the earthquake, when Wildo's father moved the family to a tent camp. Luckily, his sister was spared from that horrible experience, because her godmother took her in. Wildo was left with his father in the tent camp.

Wildo hung his head and shut down when I asked him about living in the tent camp. Shad filled in about how miserable life was after the earthquake. For example, in March 2010, Shad was handing out water to people at Wildo's tent camp. There was so much fighting that Shad needed to call the police for protection. People would steal things from the other people's tents because they could easily cut the tent fabric with a knife. In the first picture Shad took at the tent camp, Wildo was there—very skinny and malnourished—singing the Haitian national anthem.

Every time Shad visited, Wildo was there, eager to help by running errands and charming the volunteers who were visiting. Shad asked how Wildo would know that he was going to be visiting. Wildo said that any time he saw a truckload of white people, he knew Shad was in town and Wildo would be the first one to welcome the newest group of volunteers. Wildo wanted more than anything to be around Shad and his friends, because they would always have food for him. Shad learned during our interview that when Wildo went back to the tent village late at night, his dad would whip him because Wildo hadn't performed his chores that day. His dad would say that Wildo was bad and that he liked Wildo's sister better.

When Shad moved down to Haiti in July 2011, Wildo continued to visit often. One night, there was a big rainstorm. Carina and Shad decided to see what it was like in the tent camp. They found Wildo in a flooded tent, sleeping on a wooden pallet with seven other kids, and decided right then to bring all seven of them back to the shack on the roof of Shad's house, where it was dry to sleep for the night. After that, Wildo ended up staying at Shad's house—with his father's blessing.

Wildo had a crush on Carina when she first began visiting. With another volunteer's help, he made a video, singing of his love for Carina, adding in at the end, "Will you bring me a bike?" His charm was lovely as he asked with a song and a twinkle in his eye—not begging, but asking kindly for a bike. At first, when he didn't have his own bike, he would ride Carina's bike to school and—eventually—he got his own bike to run errands, get to school, and have fun.

Another boy, Danielo, was also brought into Shad's home. Danielo is four years younger than Wildo and they have learned to live like brothers, sharing a bed and chores, as well as wrestling and playing together.

What I enjoy most about Wildo is his consistently good mood. He is always ready with a smile. We invited him and Danielo to the beach one time. The car had many problems, so we had to stop many times, never making it to the beach. Wildo was sensitive to everyone's moods, doing a little dance or offering a smile when morale was low. He and Danielo seemed to have a lot of fun on what the rest of us viewed as an unsuccessful and stressful adventure. They kept us in a positive frame of mind.

Wildo told us that he would like to continue his education so that he can be an engineer and build houses, and he would like to visit New York. Wildo had the opportunity to take a photography class, which he really enjoyed, especially since he received a camera as part of participating in the class. He loves playing soccer, whether it is in the street, at recess during school, or with kids in the neighborhood. He does push-ups and runs to train for soccer, even though there is no organized coach to lead him. Wildo is on a soccer team, sponsored by Shad's cousin Reginald, which plays in the summer; they won second place in the championships. And, because Wildo has high standards for himself, he doesn't like when he misses a goal.

Wildo's Lesson: Play and Work Hard through the Challenges in Life

Wildo knew that he wanted a better life and was willing to earn it. He paid attention to what was going on around him and saw an opportunity with Shad and the volunteers. Wildo worked hard helping whenever the volunteers came, plus was a joy to be around through his entertaining attitude and dancing. People are more likely to help someone who is pleasant to be around, so Wildo was wise for being so positive and uplifting. Spending time with Wildo has taught me so much about having an optimistic attitude, plus the benefits of dancing.

Reflection

After reading Wildo's story, can you see how even in desperate situations, a person can find a way out? If you feel stuck in your circumstances, try meeting some new people and see where those connections might lead you. Are you able to open your mind to new possibilities?

Reaching for the Stars and into My Soul

Tom Blon

I bought my first telescope when I was a kid in middle school. I had a paper route, and my dad suggested that I buy a telescope. I decided to order a Celestron telescope, and contacted the company. A patient customer service lady explained that I needed cash in a checking account before I could send a check for my telescope payments. I was fortunate that this patient person helped me to get this telescope and teach me basic banking in the process.

I hosted my first astronomy night with my dad. We observed the moon and Saturn. I have checked my astronomy logbooks and I can find no record of that night, but I clearly recall the amazement both he and I expressed at those sights. Looking back, I realize that experience spurred my interest in showing the night sky to others. Seeing the moon through a scope is an eyeful—you see the craters and seas under magnification. And, if you have spent any time watching the sky, it is not a leap to reconcile the scope view of the flat grays and harsh whites and stark shadows with the lunar face you have eyed countless times. Most new moon observers will peek through the eyepiece, and then step away from the scope and compare what they saw through the telescope with what they see with unaided eye.

But Saturn, Saturn is a shock. The image of the tan dot with crescent-shaped rings on either side frequently causes first-timers to say, "No way . . . Is this fake? . . . Those are the rings?" And here is where you must trust your eyes (and the telescope) because when you step away from the eyepiece and try to find Saturn among the background stars you can see no detail—so your observation through the scope is a leap of faith.

Do you believe what the scope—and more powerful scopes, and space probes—have shown us?

The amazement my father and I both felt is one of the reasons I love teaching astronomy. Every time a star party attendee sees Jupiter for the first time and excitedly tells a parent—or an astronomy student focuses on the moon through a telescope they themselves have set up and exclaims with wonderment—I think back to the first time I saw the moon with my dad.

There are communal aspects to a star party. When we first moved to Middletown, Maria and I hosted a star party through our neighborhood watch. As the sun set, families arrived and excited children played in the yard as Mars rose in the east. We met a lot of our new neighbors for the first time. Our neighbors were willing to share their astronomy experiences. One father related that he'd watched all the Apollo launches on TV, and his son chimed in to relate some planet facts he had learned at school. One of our oldest neighborhood storytellers had binoculars in her right hand as she steadied her first telescopic view of Mars with her left hand.

A good star party host tells stories and also listens to stories. Some of the stories are ancient—constellation myths from different cultures, or star names from the Arabs—but there are new stories as well, such as the newest probe findings from Mars, or our best estimate for the age of the universe. There is a mysterious aspect to the names, the myths, and the stories the ancients told to explain the familiar rhythms of the sky, as well as the unexpected occurrences. And I clearly identify with this need to explain and document the comings and goings in the vastness of space. The darkness brings us together, and sky stories help us make sense of our own stories. Astronomy has a rich and varied past. As the oldest science, when we study the skies we participate in an activity that humans have been practicing for more than 6,000 years. I really enjoy teaching while sharing the night sky with others. I feel a bond with all the humans who have ever watched the heavens.

There are religious and spiritual aspects of astronomy, too. The history of astronomy teaches us of high priestesses and priests, the fringe visionaries who were vindicated years later. As it was so long ago, astronomic observing remains a solitary study—the lone observer in a dark field at midnight, the quiet vigils in the silent domes of mountaintop stations, and the apparition of objects foretold (by calculations). There is a sense of "apartness" from others, the feeling of being a watchman of the skies when others may be inside sealed and silent homes, with only the shifting flicker from a widescreen showing any life in the silent blocks.

Occasionally, studying the night sky, I will have doubts about how to justify the study of astronomy—how relevant is the field; are we solving the world's many problems? But I also know that it is essential for me to understand the world through our senses and reason—this is part of being human, I think—and, while observation and technology are surely tools for problem-solving, there is more . . . .

I look up at the stars and planets, awash in the human urge to explain and describe, the feeling of studying the sky by myself, on a still night, and I see old familiar sights and find objects for the first time. Then I close up my notebook, step away from the eyepiece, and look up with a resolve . . . this is a vast world, with so many unknowns, but even so, we can begin to make some sense of the world, and attempt to explain ourselves and our place in this universe.

Tom's Lesson: Sharing what I Love

The joy that Tom feels sharing his passion for astronomy is beautiful to witness. At times, astronomy is a solitary study and the astronomer is a lone observer. Instead of fearing loneliness, Tom embraces it as he shares the sense of apartness that he feels when observing. In this solitary study, Tom has found solace and passion. Sharing his love of astronomy with others reaches across boundaries and makes observing less lonely.

Reflection

When was the last time that you lay down in the grass to look up at the night sky? I welcome you to turn off your TV at night, step outside, and enjoy the light show in the sky. Is there a hobby or interest that you have had since childhood that you enjoy now or may want to revisit? Could you share your interests with people to inspire them to see the world in a little different way?

MY DREAM JOB COME TRUE
WITH A CAT ON THE COUNTER

Rae Keane

I grew up in Pittsburgh back in the early '70s—the days of hippies and love. When I was twelve, my family bought a place in the country with another family, which seemed like a perfectly normal thing to do at the time. Every weekend throughout the summer, a constant stream of people would descend on "the Farm," as it became affectionately known. We owned an eighteen-foot sailboat, and we would go sailing on Lake Wilhelm, eat massive potluck meals with our guests each providing part of the fare, wander through the woods and the fields, and sit by the campfire in the evenings and tell spooky stories while "cinder pies" stuffed with marshmallows and fruit pie fillings hissed and popped in the burning embers.

During one of these trips to the Farm, we went into the closest town—a small town called Sandy Lake. We stopped in the local hardware store for a part to fix the old water pump that was on the back porch. (The Farm did not have indoor plumbing, just the old pump that brought up frigid water with particles of rust, and an old two-seater outhouse that had an extreme pitch to the right.)

While my father was off rummaging through the dusty shelves hoping to find some hidden hardware treasure, I stayed in the front of the store eyeing up the display of licorice and horehound candies. There, lying on the worn wooden counter acting like he owned the place, was a large ginger tomcat. The cat was unperturbed by all the comings and goings around him. He turned his golden gaze toward me, and lazily stretched a paw in my direction. That was the exact moment that the thought occurred to me: someday I would like to own my own store with a cat on the counter.

Flash forward forty years . . . . I now own Zeetlegoo's Pet & People Store, a small retail pet store in the coastal town of Southport, North Carolina, complete with a store cat, Salvatore, who makes himself comfortable at the front cash register of the store. So how did I get here?

Throughout my life I have been totally indecisive as to what I wanted to do when I "grew up." I amuse myself by making lists of things I have done to make money because, unfortunately, at the end of the day there are bills to be paid. Here are just a few examples: babysitter, housekeeper, car detailer, and clerk in a sporting goods store, a hardware store, and a few clothing stores. But at the end of the day in each of those jobs, I was bored and not very challenged. I would regularly get reprimanded by my bosses for talking too much.

So at twenty-one years of age, I started college. I got an associate's degree in basic engineering, a bachelor's degree in biochemistry, and finally—after a several-year hiatus—I went back and got a master's degree in environmental science. After college, I again held many positions: polymer chemist, analytic chemist, adjunct chemistry professor, safety manager, environmental manager, and—finally—deputy public works director in a small town.

The more responsibility I got, the more money I made—and the more stressed I became. In addition, I was miserable. I would come home from my job and unload all the negativity on my husband. The other consequence of my chosen career was exposure to chemicals. During the course of my career I worked with gallons of chlorinated solvents, organic pigments, rubber vapors, and various other toxic chemicals. During the evenings, I taught chemistry lab classes and made jewelry—grinding and polishing metals. Also during this time, I had a lot of dental work done—I mean a lot. Thirteen crowns to be exact.

The result of this toxic chemical bombardment? I got sick—really sick. No one needs to hear the specifics of my various ailments, but suffice it to say that I was miserable. I had a plethora of tests run—blood tests, an upper GI, a lower GI, and a liver function test. All the tests came back with normal results. Finally, a doctor determined that since everything was testing normal, apparently I was just imagining all of my symptoms.

She suggested that I just needed to start taking anti-anxiety drugs. *Grrr-rrrr*. I knew my body and something was not right.

At that point, I started to research alternative medicines and other options. I felt awful and I knew I wasn't just imagining it. After much research, and with the help of a couple of holistic practitioners, I determined that many of my physical ailments stemmed from heavy metals that I had accumulated from years in the chemical industry, dental work, and jewelry making. A hair analysis confirmed that mercury, cadmium, and aluminum were present in my system at very high levels—and were most likely the cause of many of my symptoms.

So what does all of this have to do with starting a pet store? I am getting to that part of the story right now.

During the period of time that I was having my medical problems, my Abyssinian cat, Zeetlegoo, was also having her share of issues.

Zeetlegoo's major problem was that she vomited. Now I know you are thinking, "Well, yeah, cats do that. They are known for throwing up a hairball on occasion." But Zeetlegoo was different. Zeetlegoo was the Barfmeister—Barf-O-Matic the Cat. She would barely get her food down, and it would come right back up.

At some point while I was trying to determine what was wrong with me, I was tested for allergies. One of my trigger foods, it turned out, was corn. One day, the proverbial light bulb went off over my head when I realized that Zeetlegoo (and all other cats and dogs), like me, was unable to digest corn. In fact, I started wondering, why was I feeding a cat corn at all?

I made a trip to the grocery store and scrutinized the labels of one bag of cat food after another. I found ingredients like whole ground corn, corn gluten meal, and corn syrup. I had spent many years taking biology courses, and yet it hadn't occurred to me that I was feeding an obligate carnivore a highly indigestible grain—and that this was causing the poor cat to be given unflattering nicknames due to her behavior.

We finally found a brand of cat food that was a premium holistic food—with no corn, wheat, soy, by-products, or preservatives. Unfortunately, we had to drive twenty-five miles up to the city of Wilmington to get the food. Our other option? Driving twenty-five miles to the south.

We had recently moved from the Piedmont of North Carolina to the small coastal town of Southport, because I had taken a job as deputy public works director for a local town. My husband Paul was finishing up a nine-month contract with his employer in Greensboro—spending a week in Greensboro, and then a week in Southport. For years, I had talked about starting my own business, so prior to the end of his contract, we started researching established businesses that were for sale in the area.

We didn't really have any direction; in fact, we looked at a tool rental company since I had worked at a hardware store for thirteen years. Then we found a local pet store that was on the market—the name, the inventory, and the building. Although I had never owned a dog, and Paul had never worked in retail, we decided that we both liked animals, and that pets make people happy. The price of the shop seemed high, but working with a commercial realtor, we put in an offer. And our offer was rejected. No counteroffer—nothing.

Since we were planning to start our own business, we were working with a lawyer to incorporate. Even though we weren't sure exactly what business we were going to start, we knew legally it was best to incorporate. During a meeting with the lawyer, we mentioned the pet store offer. The lawyer said, "Did you like the name of the business?" Paul and I looked at one another shaking our heads . . . "No," we both said. "Did you like the inventory that they had in stock?" Again Paul and I looked at one another. "No," we exclaimed simultaneously. "How about the building and its location?" questioned the lawyer. "Not really . . . ," I said. "So why would you spend a considerable amount of money to get something you don't want in a business you aren't sure you are going to like?" the lawyer remarked. "Why don't you rent a place and start your own business the way you want it?" That was probably the best $250 we ever spent, because that is exactly what we did.

Working with the same realtor, we found a storefront in an excellent location with good parking. The building was brand new, so my husband, acting as subcontractor, outfitted the building—putting in walls, drop ceilings, and store fixtures, which we had been lucky enough to find second-hand. The name of the business was easy; we named it after our inspiration for the store: the barfing cat Zeetlegoo.

In December 2004, Zeetlegoo's Pet & People Store opened its doors. For the first couple months, my husband ran the store, while I continued to work full time at the town, placing orders in the evenings and helping at the store on Saturdays. We joined the local Chamber of Commerce and had a grand opening which Zeetlegoo, now sixteen and starting to get frail, attended—my very own retail establishment with a cat.

After four months, I decided that I could no longer take the negative atmosphere of my job. I called my husband and we decided that my health and sanity were more important than a paycheck, so despite the fact that the store had only been open a short time, we agreed that I should resign from my position. We didn't know if we were going to make it in business, or even when we would be able to pay ourselves. Nonetheless, April Fool's Day of 2005 was my last day of working for "the Man."

We lived primarily on savings for two years, during which Paul and I worked a ridiculous number of hours every week. And I flourished in this atmosphere. I could sit at my computer at two in the morning in my pajamas and order dog toys . . . with no one to tell me what to do and when. I could stand around and gab with customers for as long as I wanted. I was finally the boss.

And the myriad jobs that I held through the years—as well as my biochemistry knowledge and my love of pets and people—helped to create a store unlike any other, offering only top-of-the-line products, especially focusing on healthy foods for the animals. In 2006, Sammy cat came and made himself at home in the store and became the first store cat. In addition to employing felines, we have had two canines who have diligently worked doing demonstrations, tasting treats, testing toys, and greeting customers.

This year, Zeetlegoo's Pet & People Store is celebrating ten years in business. We have five full-time and three part-time employees, are open seven days a week (although Paul and I have a much reduced work schedule), and have won "Best Pet Store in Brunswick County" for all six years that the contest has been held. I still work from home in my pajamas and still love my job. And Salvatore the cat sits on the store counter . . .

Rae's Lesson: Continuing to Search for my Perfect Job

Rae's story is great because she shares the many different careers she tried, searching for what she might really enjoy. I imagine many people feeling similar to Rae, not quite sure what they want to do when they "grow up." Rae paid attention to clues along the way, knowing that someday she wanted a store with a cat on the counter. The combination of her illness and that of her cat Zeetlegoo, the Barfmeister, actually helped Rae to find her way to the career that she loves, which is owning Zeetlegoo's Pet & People Store. When we are in the middle of life's biggest challenges, they seem like so much trouble and feel pointless. Yet often, in retrospect, the challenges served a purpose. Reading Rae's story and reflecting on the series of events which led her to find her passion, I feel like she was being guided to finding the job that she truly loves.

Reflection

What clues have you noticed as to what catches your eye, feels right, or strikes your fancy? Is there a dream that you have had since you were a child that might be valuable to explore? Allow yourself time to explore many different options. As you read long ago in my chapter, I needed to take time to experiment with many different jobs before I honed in on writing and speaking.

Many businesses fail due to lack of research and planning. What steps should you take to make your dream job a reality? Building a support team of people to help you with different aspects of your business is key. For example, the lawyer that Rae and Paul met with before choosing their location gave them much-needed and helpful advice. Consider preparing your new business while you are working at your current job. As you gain experience and success, you can phase into your new business, while building your confidence.

CLOSING REMARKS

Maria Blon

So here we are at the conclusion of this book filled with stories of people who have shown you how they embraced challenges and found purpose, meaning, and passion in their lives. You probably have found favorite stories that touched your heart because—in some ways—you have lived those stories in your own life. Over time, the stories that can best offer you guidance may change as you evolve and embrace the continual flow of the LOVE Formula:

> **Let go...**
> **Open your mind**
> **Vision**
> **Experience Everything**

You may get frustrated if a challenge you thought you had overcome rears its ugly head yet again, maybe in a slightly different form. I invite you to look at repeat challenges as practice, testing if you have fully learned the lesson presented.

Time after time, each of these authors have taken their individual life challenges and solved them by reaching out and helping a bigger circle of people. In that process, they have gained so much, helping themselves and many people along the way. Follow these inspiring author's leads by looking inside to find what is important to you, then reaching out to help in a bigger and more fulfilling way. You will bring great meaning and joy to your life and the lives of countless people.

Imagine how Shad's life and everyone's lives would be different if he had returned to the United States when the future of the HEART School seemed dismal, at best. Shad learned that perseverance paid off.

Imagine if Rosita chose to be bitter about all of the obstacles in her way as she was trying to make a better life for herself and her children. Instead, Rosita uses laughter to keep her spirits up, bringing joy and hope to everyone around her.

Imagine if Sheila had never mustered the chutzpa to write that letter to the President of the congregation where she didn't get the job she knew she was destined to have, explaining they made the wrong choice. She wouldn't have received this call from the President: "Sheila... you were right...we did make a mistake...are you still available?" Sheila's courage to boldly share her feelings after being rejected teaches us that following our passion may take a lot of guts, but the rewards are amazing.

I encourage you to have compassion for yourself on your journey, taking time to heal and learn from the lessons in this book, then doing what feels exciting and right for you. Reach out to help first with small steps, then with confidence reaching out more. You may be surprised by how inspired you feel and how people around you admire your courage to follow your passion.

We would love to hear your stories at: PeopleLivingPassionately. com and facebook.com/sparksalive. Since life is ever changing, don't be surprised if you speak to us after this book is published and we are doing something new. After all, as Peggy says so beautifully, we are each a "work in progress."

May SPARKS of passion guide your days,
while specks of worry float away!

Author Biographies

Enjoy reading about our authors.
You might also like seeing our pictures at
PeopleLivingPassionately.com.

Dr. Ivan Misner is the Founder & Chairman of BNI, the world's largest business networking organization. BNI was founded in 1985. The organization now has over 6,700 chapters throughout every populated continent of the world. Last year alone, BNI generated 5.4 million referrals resulting in over $6.5 billion dollars' worth of business for its members. Dr. Misner is a *New York Times* Bestselling author who has written 19 books including his latest release; *Who's In Your Room? (2014)* Dr. Misner was recently named "*Humanitarian of the Year*" by the Red Cross. He and his wife, Elisabeth, are now "empty nesters" with three adult children — *Oh, and in his spare time!!!* he is also an amateur magician and a black belt in karate. Dr. Misner's websites include IvanMisner.com, BNI.com, BNIFoundation.org and MisnerPlan.com.

Maria Blon is an international speaker and author with her company SPARKS! Maria began her professional life as a holistic math teacher at the community college level, teaching students and future teachers to love mathematics through hands-on, interactive learning. Maria's life has transformed at a number of different times in her life, most especially when she and her daughter volunteered in Haiti after the devastating earthquake of 2010. Maria helped start the HEART School in Haiti, where she has trained the teachers and is the secretary and co-president of the HEART Board. Maria loves to engage and inspire her audience throughout her presentations and is thrilled to be the coordinating author for this book. Contact Maria through her websites: Sparksalive.com and PeopleLivingPassionately.com.

Peggy Gilbart is our story editor. She has been an educator in public and private schools for most of her professional life, as well as an author of science textbook supplements. Currently, in addition to providing editing services, she is working at a local artisan distillery, helping to produce beautiful, high quality brandies, and is an avid photographer and quilter. She lives in the Quiet Corner area of Connecticut with her family. For editing inquiries, Peggy can be reached at gentle.editing@gmail.com.

Alison Orlando is a certified health coach with Take Shape For Life; she is certified by the MacDonald Center for Obesity Prevention and Education at the College of Nursing, Villanova University, and holds a master's degree in education from Fordham University. She is a board member of the Andy K & Friends Charitable Foundation, president of the BNI chapter of Warwick, New York, and a New York State certified school counselor. Alison lives in New York with her husband, Michael, and children, William and Abigail. You may reach out to Alison at AlisonOrlando.TSFL.com.

Deborah Cohen began her highly successful coaching career as a midwife! For the last fifteen years, Deborah has effectively coached individuals and large groups for Landmark Education, a noted leader in the personal growth and development industry. With a master's of science in community health nursing, thirty years of experience in mental health nursing and forty years of experience in alternative and holistic healing modalities. Deborah brings the best of all worlds to her private coaching practice. She dances with the rigors of science and the vision of new horizons. You may connect with Deborah at deblifecoach.com. You may also find her out dancing, swing, salsa, zydeco... ask her! She'd love to dance with you!

Wendy Blanchard, M.S., is a writer for her companies, The Rx Diaries, and Blissfully Gl-Airy Free, and a radio host of her show, The Rx Diaries, on IntentionRadio.com. Wendy is raising awareness, and educating and empowering others, through a "clean and green lifestyle, one day at a time." Wendy is a retired teacher and business owner, and lives in New York. She has three children, and one granddaughter. You may reach Wendy at therxdiaries.com, blissfullyglairyfree.com, and intentionradio.com/rx.

Sue Keane holds various volunteer positions, including delivering food through the Meals on Wheels program, assisting with the altar guild for St Andrews Episcopal Church, preparing taxes for families in low-income areas, mailing letters for the HEART School in Haiti, and maintaining Bullocks Pen Park, where she walks her dog, Ivie. Sue has three children: Maria, Paul, and Evan; and two grandchildren: Carina and Anna.

Carina Blon spent two and a half years with the HEART School in Haiti, then moved back to her hometown of Middletown, New York to attend college full time.   She is majoring in Human and Community Services through Empire State College and has been volunteering and working for local human service agencies since her move back in January 2014. Carina continues to serve on the HEART board as Community Liaison, coordinating Buddy Program correspondences, cross cultural learning exchanges between the US and the school in Haiti, and continuing to support teacher, staff and community efforts on the ground in Haiti. Carina can be reached at carina@heartinhaiti.org.

Shad St Louis is the founder, director of operations, and co-president of the HEART school (Ecole Mixte des Sibert) in Haiti. Shad organized fundraising and on-site relief help for the Katrina relief effort in 2005. He has worked as a guidance counselor, youth mentor, and transfer counselor in New York, where he is now living. Learn more about the HEART school at heartinhaiti.org.

Melanie Wood, PRYT-P, practices Personal Integration, a modality that offers you an innovative approach to challenges in your ever-changing life. Melanie developed Personal Integration by combining her studies in psychology with her extensive training, experience, and personal practice of yoga, Phoenix Rising yoga therapy, meditation, and spirituality. Melanie earned her bachelor's degree from Ashford College and her master's degree from Burlington College. She is an adjunct professor of graduate classes at Burlington College and undergraduate classes at Corning Community College. You may contact Melanie at facebook. com/PersonalIntegration.

Sheila Pearl is an international author, speaker, and relationship coach. She is a multi-faceted professional: a retired cantor and educator, a clinical social worker, certified life coach, and family therapist. She has been in private practice for over thirty years, working with clients in her office and globally via Skype and phone. Sheila is the author of *Ageless & Sexy: Loving Relationships in Mid-Life* and co-author of the bestselling book *Pearls of Wisdom: 30 Inspirational Ideas for Your Best Life Now (2012)* with Jack Canfield and Marci Shimoff, as well as being one of the contributors to *Wake Up Women! BE Happy, Healthy & Wealthy: A Guidebook (2008)*. You may connect with Sheila at SheilaPearl.com and AgelessAndSexyBook.com.

Anna Blon is currently studying psychology at the College of Saint Rose. She cheers for both the men's and women's basketball teams. Her interests include shopping at thrift stores, baking, hiking, and traveling.

Rev. Dechen Rheault is a gifted seer, empathic, and energy healer with clients spanning the globe. She is a licensed ordained interfaith minister, body-mind therapist, educator, poet, and songwriter. With a passion to serve, she has sat on many non-profit boards and, through her work with the elderly, was a recipient of the Governor's Healthy Aging Award in Vermont. You may contact Dechen at yourwisdomways.com.

Brian K. Baird is an architect of change. With thirty-five years as an entrepreneur and sales leader, Brian walked away from corporate America because he saw the tremendous need to empower individuals to align their life span, health span, and wealth span so they don't outlive their health and money. Recently, he has been working with charities and non-profit community organizations to harness exciting new ideas in fundraising, thus increasing his reach in changing people's lives. He started his journey with a stint in the US Naval Nuclear Propulsion Program, followed by a bachelor of science degree from Hofstra University and three years modeling data for Wall Street. His other passions include spending quality time with his beautiful wife and brilliant, teen-aged daughter. You can reach Brian at TheEffectiveWay.com.

Jean Widletson Gaspard attends the third grade at the HEART school in Haiti. He eagerly volunteers to help the preschool children by mentoring them, playing with them, and walking them to the cafeteria for lunch. He also likes helping his mother at home. Jean enjoys learning about growing plants for both food and medicine.

Anthony Church is a passionate lifelong entrepreneur who has built and run several companies including Custom Cover Productions, High Performance Active Wear, Hudson Valley Pet Store, and Blue Buckle Marketing. He earned his bachelor's degree in psychology and master's degree in business management from SUNY New Paltz, in New York, and is currently working on a number of exciting new projects. He has created the "I am Jean Elie" project, which helps raise money to fight the effects of hunger and malnutrition around the world. Please find out more about him at anthonychurchonline.com and IamJeanElie. com.

Charles Yarnold, vice president of Focused Wealth Management, is an SEC-registered investment advisor. He is a co-founder of the River-View Run for Parkinson's research, is an active runner and fundraiser for Team Fox, and member of the Michael J. Fox Foundation. Charles also is on the board of Caring Connections, a not-for-profit organization that serves as a resource for the caregivers of Ulster County. Charles was an all-decade pitcher on the Rensselaer Polytechnic Institute baseball team. You may contact Charles at FocusedWealthMgmt. com

Rosita Labousse leads the kitchen staff at the HEART school in Haiti. She lives across from the school in Merger, Croix-des-Bouquets, with her six children, dogs, cats, pigs, and chickens. Rosita worked as a care aid for an orphanage in Haiti and still keeps in touch with the children there. Rosita has taken many continuing education classes and advocates for all children to earn an education.

Vilma Fyke is an energy healer who uses a number of techniques to get to the root of dis-ease in order to bring forth greater health and well-being. Through her company Positive Alternatives, Vilma offers Electro Physiological Biofeedback, Rife and Bio Cleanse Foot Bath, Isometric Muscle Balancing, Health Kinesiology and Total Body Modification, to name a few of her services.

Dr. Bradley Nelson is the developer of the most advanced form of energy medicine on the planet. A holistic chiropractic physician and medical intuitive, Dr. Nelson is one of the world's foremost experts in the emerging fields of bioenergetic medicine and energy psychology. His bestselling book, *The Emotion Code*, is helping people all over the world to improve their lives by ridding themselves of their imbalancing emotional baggage. Learn more at Dr. Bradley Nelson's website HealersLibrary.com.

Wildo Bruny is a student at La Providence de Sibert. He loves playing soccer, dancing, spending time with his friends, and learning English. Wildo is always willing to advocate for people in need.

Tom Blon teaches physics at Middletown High School and astronomy at Orange County Community College. He continues to expand his education with courses including interesting topics of black holes, telescopes, human centrifuge, and plasma, to name a few. Tom earned his bachelor's degree in science from Penn State University and his master's degree from City University of New York. Tom served in the United States Navy for five years, sailing to the west coast of Africa, the Mediterranean, and around South America. He lives with his wife, Maria, daughters, Carina and Anna, and dog, Lilli, in New York.

Rae Keane is a native of Pittsburgh, PA, but has settled in North Carolina where she and her husband run Zeetlegoo's Pet & People Store in the small coastal town of Southport. Rae has an undergraduate degree in Biochemistry and a Master's degree in Environmental Science, but she was unhappy trying to climb the corporate ladder. After many years of job changes and unsatisfying career choices she took a chance and opened the store of her dreams - a pet supply store that only carries healthy foods and treats and a tremendous selection of unique pet products... complete with a cat on the counter. Zeetlegoo's is now entering their 10th year in business and has won many accolades including various customer service awards and seven time winner of Best Pet Store in Brunswick County. Visit our website at Zeetlegoos.com.

Acknowledgments

Over 20 years ago, I clearly remember talking with Peggy about visionaries like Martin Luther King, Mother Theresa, Nelson Mandela and Mahatma Gandhi, wondering how they could be so selfless, peaceful and inspiring while helping billions of people. Peggy explained that all great people have a large and strong support network, which helped them to reach so many people. I can easily understand how this is true because even with this relatively small project of collaborating to create this book, I have received so much support.

First and foremost thank you, the reader, for selecting this book and taking time to read our stories. I hope that you have received at least a few valuable insights that will help you to live passionately, inspiring many on your journey. I have so much appreciation for each of our co-authors who have bravely shared their intimate story, given much valuable feedback, cheered me on and joined in this publishing process by answering my many questions and requests. I have so much gratitude to Peggy for your patient, wise guidance and editing over many years. To the people who live in our house: Tom, Carina, Anna and Shad, thank you for your support and patience, especially since my favorite topic of discussion has often been this book. Mom and Dad, thank you for your encouragement and giving me a life with many opportunities for adventure. Paul, thank you for leading our family in entrepreneurism and helping me along the way. Evan, thanks for being the reason that I got my first keynote speaking job. I have learned so much from you. I hope that you are happy being reunited with Dad in heaven.

Many thanks to my great friend Pam McMahon. Your careful listening, genuine interest in and encouragement with every new adventure has been invaluable. I am so lucky to have you right across the street! Jane Harrington, you were my first client when I took this leap of faith to venture out on my own, which I so appreciate. We have had great fun on our adventures, especially conquering Mount Marcy, even when they said we couldn't do it. Chrissy Fulciniti, thank you for being my yoga teacher for so many years, helping me to gain strength and flexibility.

To my friends and colleagues at SUNY Orange, thank you for inspiring me with your teaching and leadership: Elizabeth Tarvin, Michelle Tubbs, Eileen Burke, Shelly Paradies, Ann Ruscher, Karen Stephens and Jennifer Merriam. I loved the beautiful party you gave me when I left the college to begin my entrepreneurial adventures!

I have so much gratitude for Anthony Church, who has encouraged and guided me through this entire process. How lucky I am to have you as my marketing coach because I can tell you I am terrified and you understand completely, then give me small steps to courageously keep going. Thanks to your team at Blue Buckle and Interact Marketing: Joe Beccalori for helping to create the marketing plan and to Tyler DeVogel for designing our beautiful cover!

Marianne Sciucco, bestselling author of *Blue Hydrangeas (2013)* has been an inspiration, an approachable role model in the publishing world and offered me much needed advice about writing, publishing and marketing. Marianne taught me the joy of rewriting, editing and continuing to improve my descriptions. She was one of only two people who attended the very first class that Ann Bell and I taught using our Inspiration Cards. I can't even begin to describe how very much that meant to me.

Emil Reyes, thank you for reading me your beautifully crafted stories so that I could learn how to bravely share my feelings with readers. I look forward to seeing your books in print soon! I appreciate the time you took from your busy schedule to give me helpful feedback on enriching my story.

Many thanks to Two Harbors Press, whose staff has given us the opportunity to become a bestseller through your traditional publishing expertise, yet self-publishing empowerment. You all have guided me to bump up the professionalism several notches, for which I am very appreciative. I ask lots of questions and thank you for your patience. I am thrilled that you have made it possible for us to publish in the most sustainable manner with soy-based ink.

Dr. Ivan Misner, thank you for:

- Creating and growing BNI (Business Network International) because through this organization, I have learned how to grow my business using your beautiful *Givers Gain*

Philosophy. I would have been very lost without the support of my local BNI Profit Makers chapter, Frank DeRaffele's Entrepreneurial Excellence classes and the vast network that you have created.

- Writing such a beautiful foreword for this book. I don't know how to express in words what an incredible boost I have felt receiving your support. When I noticed doubt creeping in during this process, I remembered that we had your endorsement as a New York Times Bestselling author, and I renewed my hope that we could follow in your footsteps.

- Being a role model of an effective entrepreneur, healer and humanitarian who is helping people around the world through your inspiring leadership.

- Sharing our book with your followers so that we can help as many people as possible.

Thank you Frank DeRaffele for being our regional director of the Hudson Valley BNI and for asking Dr. Ivan Misner to write our foreword. Many thanks to members of my BNI Profit Makers group: Alison Orlando (Take Shape for Life), Anthony Church (Bluebuckle Marketing), Brian Baird (The Effective Way), Charles Yarnold (Focused Wealth Management), Michelle Dixon (Seely and Durland Insurance), David Cosco (Home Bridge Financial Services), Erni Hewett (Erni Girl Designs), Ron Alindogan (Floor Coverings International), George Tuttle (Certa Pro Painters), Monte Morris (A Green CPA), Greg Miller (CMIT Solutions), Andrea Volter (Design Concepts), Tara Diffenbach, Kevin Mulqueen (New York Life Insurance), Jacqueline Kraszewski (The Green Team Home Selling System), Walter Popailo (Jesters Comedy Club), Ingrid Lucas (Lucas Speech Pathology), Charlie Skerett (Starlight Entertainment), Jeannie-Marie Lowell (Pampered Chef). Week after week you have laughed at my antics and encouraged me to be the best person that I can be. Here is a poem sharing how I feel about all of you:

A fiercely independent person
searching to find her way.

To be herself, yet feel supported
through each and every day.

Her drive to keep evolving
has pushed some away.

But there is one group who
embraces her joyful play.

Many thanks to the BNI Profit Makers
for your encouragement every Thursday!

Thank you to all of the angels in heaven and on earth who
are guiding us on this amazing life journey!